CONTEMPORARY FRENCH WOMEN POETS

Chiasma 2

General Editor

Michael Bishop

Editorial Committee

Adelaide Russo, Michael Sheringham
Steven Winspur, Sonya Stevens
Michael Brophy

AMSTERDAM - ATLANTA, GA 1995

Michael Bishop

CONTEMPORARY
FRENCH WOMEN POETS

Volume 1
from
Chedid and Dohollau
to
Tellermann and Bancquart

♾ Le papier sur lequel le présent ouvrage est imprimé remplit les prescriptions de "ISO 9706:1994, Information et documentation - Papier pour
documents - Prescriptions pour la permanence".

♾ The paper on which this book is printed meets the requirements of "ISO
9706:1994, Information and documentation - Paper for documents -
Requirements for permanence".

ISBN: 90-5183-844-1 (CIP)
©Editions Rodopi B.V., Amsterdam - Atlanta, GA 1995
Printed in The Netherlands

CHIASMA

Chiasma seeks to foster urgent critical assessments focussing upon joinings and criss-crossings, single, triangular, multiple, in the realm of modern French literature. Studies may be of an interdisciplinary nature, developing connections with art, philosophy, linguistics and beyond, or display intertextual or other univocal concerns of varying order.

*

CONTENTS

Acknowledgements

I should like to acknowledge the generous support of the Social Sciences and Humanities Research Council of Canada which has greatly facilitated the completion of this book and its companion volume. My very great thanks go to all the writers whose work is discussed here, for their encouragement and assistance in endless matters. And my profoundest thanks are reserved for Colette whose intelligence and sensitivity are boundless.

*

for Colette,

Nadine, Katherine, Danai and Sophie

*

SOME PRELIMINARY REMARKS

"Ici notre faim et notre fête"
Françoise Hàn

*

"Et si la règle s'altère?"
Esther Tellermann

*

"O ma matrie désaffectée"
Jeanne Hyvrard

I

To have reached the point, after years of reading, reflection and writing, where, finally, it is possible to prepare an Introduction to both the eight studies that this volume offers and, implicitly, the eight, equally completed and to follow in volume II--to have reached this point is not--I only now have come to sense this--without its delicacy and a certain intrinsic difficulty. Any difficulty, however, I hope to dispel by proceeding straightforwardly and honestly. My preliminary remarks will thus, briefly, relate the gestation of this book, its companion volume and other work to come; acknowledge my indebtedness to many; endeavour to spell out what the book, and again its companion, seek to accomplish, or not accomplish; provide a telescoped sense of both my general view of poetry's pertinences and what I feel are some of the global, chiasmically interpertinent features to watch out for in the complex and infinitely facetted individual *oeuvres* of the eight women poets discussed in volume I of *Contemporary French Women Poets*.

My earlier university studies were not remarkable for their insistence upon women's writing and it took the close subsequent exchanges with students in classes for which I had teaching responsibility, as well as the consciousness-raising allowed by my privileged relationships with Colette, my wife, and our daughters, to generate the extra energy required to uncover that teeming feminine poetic and literary activity still largely occulted by even careful scrutiny of major bibliographies, repertories of books in print and so on. Although French literary production as a whole suffers from this occultation--a result of publishing policies, poor publicity and dissemination, indifferent media coverage, academic conservatism and anachronism--, poetry is particularly affected. Consciousness of the very existence of women's poetical works in the modern and contemporary field in France is often extremely limited, even amongst writers themselves. My own efforts--after earlier research resulting in books and numerous essays on the contemporary poetry of France, all of which confirmed the great unavailability of work by women poets and consequent absence of critical response--were simple and practical, and bore immediate fruits for all of my teaching: I wrote to all those poets and writers I knew in France, and all critics I knew in the modern French poetry field. The results both exemplified the problem and resolved it: Yves Bonnefoy expressed his admiration for Heather Dohollau and Martine Broda; André Frénaud suggested exploring Marie Etienne; and so on--one name here, two there, except for Bernard Noël with his prolific and sharp awareness. My slowly developed contacts with the women poets themselves were, however, as one might imagine, determining and the generosity and scrupulously attentive assistance of Anne Teyssiéras, in particular, but many other women writers in important degrees, soon enabled me to map out a programme of reading enough to last a few years. Soon, moreover, my list of poets had grown to twenty; today it contains over forty-five names, all contemporary, and expands each year. Systematic incorporation of a considerable selection of this poetry into literature programmes thus profoundly rethought and rebalanced has brought me, and, I believe, many students, great personal benefit and joy. My own life, to the extent it is consciousness and sensibility in action, has been significantly transformed for the good. Vast, new realms of experience, vision and feasibility have opened up, and this, despite the fact that I had already read women such as Beauvoir, Wittig, Cixous, Chawaf or Irigaray.

II

I have already hinted at my indebtedness to many colleagues and, especially, women poets during the initial phase of establishing the immense corpus that contemporary women's poetry amazingly constitutes. The present volume and that about to "complete" it require, however, that I express my very considerable thanks to all of the poets therein discussed: Andrée Chedid, Heather Dohollau, Denise Le Dantec, Janine Mitaud, Jacqueline Risset, Anne Teyssiéras, Esther Tellermann and Marie-Claire Bancquart for volume I; Jeanne Hyvrard, Jeannine Baude, Françoise Hàn, Céline Zins, Vénus Khoury-Ghata, Denise Borias, Marie Etienne and Anne-Marie Albiach for volume II. Without their often remarkable kindnesses, their moral and material support in the provision of books, manuscripts, inédits, their exchange of ideas, their patience with certain requests for information, their simple human generosities--without all this, and more, it would have been impossible to achieve even the small accomplishment that, I hope, the study of these sixteen very fine poets will be seen to represent. Moreover, let me stress just how difficult my final choice of poets was, putting aside even my desire to focus upon work of the past thirty years especially. If I could thus somewhat justify,

9

from a strictly temporal point of view, the omission of powerful poetic voices such as those of Angèle Vannier, Pierrette Sartin, Claudine Chonez and Marie-Jeanne Durry, and if I could argue the omission, on the grounds of J. H. Matthews' elegant full-length study, of the inimitable Joyce Mansour, it was nevertheless difficult to exclude, for reasons of space and in the light of my perceived need to offer the fullest sense of the range of mode and consciousness, poets such as Claude de Burine with her ever-astonishing imagery and biting sensuality, Martine Broda with the skeletal shrewdness of her just collected work (*Grand jour*, 1994), Yvonne Caroutch and her quasi-mystical, half-mythical yet firmly anchored urgencies, Hélène Cadou with her haunting hauntedness and her moving patience, Sylvia Baron Supervielle and her elliptical condensations lived and written with, "sur ma face / un éventail de fumée". These and other poets have often shown similar generosity towards me in my research and, above all, the value, the quality of their work, its extensiveness, merit an attention the present studies simply cannot provide. Certain efforts elsewhere, in reviews, essays and papers given or to come, help remedy such frustration on my part, and, perhaps most importantly a critical bilingual anthology of contemporary women's poetry in France will serve, as well as the present studies, to encourage many others to seek the pleasure and enlightenment that have come my way--an anthology inspired by the excellent work of Jeanine Moulin and work such as that of Jean Breton with *Poésie 1*, but significantly different from, say, the albeit fine anthologising fervours of Michel Décaudin (*Anthologie de la poésie française du XXe siècle*) or Henri Deluy (*La Poésie en France, 1983-1988: une anthologie critique*).

III

Some of my specific aims in writing these two books will be reasonably apparent at this point, but I should like, nevertheless, to be more explicit and make clear, too, what the volumes do not seek to accomplish. My first concern is to share my pleasures and discoveries in the simplest manner possible. Volume I and Volume II both seek to recognise, to honour and unpretentiously, untendentiously reveal and discuss in a broad, preliminary manner, poetic work of high quality and human pertinence. It is my hope that other critics and students of contemporary literature will thus be encouraged to read and explore the work of these sixteen women, and perhaps feel some companionship in at times quite uncharted waters. I have tried to expose, in the two volumes taken together, the fullest *range* possible of *individual* poetic endeavours, whilst allowing to emerge, often more implicitly than explicitly and via brief allusive flourish, cross-pertinence from woman to woman or poet to poet, and historical depth and perspective, whereby given *œuvres* may be seen in the optic of both the larger contemporary French poetic tradition and the specifically feminine heritage running from Marie de France, Christine de Pisan, Pernette du Guillet and Louise Labé to poets such as Claire Goll, Marie Noël, Louise de Vilmorin, Anna de Noailles, Catherine Pozzi, surrealists such as Rahon and Penrose, pacifists such as Léonie Sourd and Henriette Sauret. I stress, such efforts are concise, parenthetical, ellipses whose fuller or lesser significance these studies cannot tease out. There is, moreover, no strategic positioning. Whilst, in effect, I endeavour to remain alert to new, newly voiced, newly envisioned factors, it should be remembered that, in a *certain* sense, beyond history and tradition, this book, with its companion volume, exists precisely because *everything* here is new, original, streamingly revealed herstory, a *poiesis* of many, largely occulted feminine consciousnesses. My aim is never to appropriate, but simply to learn from the latter; not to stabilise or systematise, and still less to methodologise, but to remain ever sensitive to the intrinsic and remarkable otherness of each poetic voice. I do not lay, cannot lay, any claim to gynesis, gynocriticism or feminism, whilst remaining utterly sympathetic to such readings in a world still massively oppressing physically and psychologically, spiritually, over two billion women. There may be clumsinesses. I hope they are infrequent. They are certainly not part of any programme. All the poets discussed have given me much support and confidence in this regard, and I thank them, once again, for this significant gift, over and above that of their work itself. My purpose, then, from beginning to end, has been simple: to listen, and to share some things heard, felt, thought, so that many more listenings may occur.

I have offered some observations already on the "chiasmic" nature of the twin volumes of *Contemporary French Women Poets*. The emphasis given, as I ever prefer to give it, to the specificity of individual *œuvres* does not permit a constant, flagrant collation of factors, nor the development of an overall, central thesis of intersection and cross-weaving. Nevertheless, much that is chiasmic remains: the juxtaposition and inherently parallel, interconnected revelation of sixteen contemporary poetic modes and sixteen contemporary feminine consciousnesses, with their overlapping socio-political, ethico-spiritual, psychological and aesthetic concerns and visions. To the question "Are there global models to be constructed here?", these two volumes answer only elliptically. Much is dealt with that would allow for such construction and both the final part of this Introduction--very gingerly--and the conclusions to the two volumes evoke factors that can be greatly amplified by means of more specifically oriented inquiry. Much would depend upon the type of chiasma one might initially posit as significant, of interest. And herein lies my own mild reservation about the critical development of global, tightly chiasmic analysis--and my preference for the lightly allusive, elliptically implicit, the rather furtive "chiasmic" approach *Contemporary French Women Poets* adopts. Moreover, one last fact supports, I believe, my preference for a tender modulation of the individual, the specific, and the cross-referentially theoretical, the chiasmic: my own thinking about the sixteen women poets dealt with here remains in its very, very early days. Perhaps in the light of further studies, by others, over time, firmer networking and chiasmic analysis will be inspired. Certainly, there is much more food for thought in the rich poetic *œuvres* discussed here.

IV

A very brief word about certain aspects of my approach that are not already evident may not be unhelpful. I have presented individual *œuvres* chronologically, seeking to show the consistent and changing patterns of both consciousness and modal conveyance. If not all collections of one or two poets are dealt with, completeness tends largely to reign, except for a few titles received at the proof stage. Global assessments of these chronologically analysed collections are given, some relatively compact, others more ample, this dependent upon factors of prolificness, complexity, length, originality and so on--not to mention constraints of space upon me. The compact global assessment is frequently wedded to textual analysis, with or without full citation of the poem under scrutiny, and again of different intensity and insistence. Of primary pertinence to me, as will already be reasonably clear, is my sense of the psychological, ethical, socio-political, spiritual and aesthetic elements at play in given

13

collections and representative poems--the complex consciousness of human, and inevitably specifically feminine, presence in the world. If I remain sensitive to formal, stylistic features, it is not in an endeavour to privilege them over ontological, existential parameters--far from it: the issues of being and presence far outweigh, to my mind, the niceties of form. But my aim is not to prejudge even here; and, in certain cases, the relationship between form and vastly pertinent and teeming questions of language is manifestly subtle and worthy of the most intimate analysis-- which, whilst not always feasible here, at least can seek its springboard. If, then, as I shall again suggest in the last of these preliminary remarks, poetic form and aestheticised textual interiority and closure are not the primary foci of all of the women poets discussed, and if, then, rather, what dominates is, precisely, the psychological, the ethical, the spiritual, the sociological--then this suits me very well. Language remains central, but as an ethical, spiritual or political factor. Aesthetics is always a matter of deep visceral and cosmic significance, not a place of idle play or dry intellectualness.

V

What, then, in brief, can I suggest the reader remain alert to in respect of the shared, chiasmically pertinent features driving the work of the eight women poets treated in volume I? Firstly, and perhaps centrally, there is the issue already evoked of the privileging of the urgencies of existential and ontological consciousness over the temptations of an intellection of purely formal, modal, ludic pertinence. Secondly, and in consequence, concept tends, *toutes proportions gardées*, to take a back seat to experience. Thirdly, and once again one can easily follow the slope of these shared tendencies, there is a common and heightened sensitivity o the delicate and shifting, but ever central relationships of self to world, o the other: trees, earth, light, sea, people known, people seemingly remote, children, lovers, strangers, those at ease, those in turmoil and oppressed. "Monde je suis mêlée à toi", writes Janine Mitaud, "dans le ruissellement torrentiel des planètes" (EC, 26). Fourthly, one could meditate fruitfully upon a whole criss-crossing poetics of the sensed otherness of the self: the pertinence of body, of sensual and sexual experience, their beauties and their traumas, plunged as they are into questions of sociality, ethics, human or specifically feminine value. In this joint context of self-other and self-self relations, and fifthly, many factors remain to be weighed: closeness and distance; compassion, love, self-esteem, and violence, appropriation; nostalgic memory or vision, and loss, absence, death; the absurd and the "uncertainty of derision", as Marie-Claire Bancquart writes (OO, 64), even a persistent sense of a divineness beyond all dogma; the tensions of void and meaning that Denise Borias characteristically voices (PF, 49); "difference" and "fusion", as Jeanne Hyvrard might say, integrity and connectedness. Sixthly, whilst certain poets inevitably write tensionally and whilst anguish can flash or persist, all poets are astonishingly resilient, all eight *œuvres* can reveal much serenity, surging simple joys, a sense of grace. Further, it is a seventh element to explore intertextually, there is little prescription, little proscription amongst these eight women. On the other hand, if isms fade in the face of open meditation of experience, vigour abounds; not-knowing can be a mightily positive force, as with a Marguerite Duras or an Anne-Marie Albiach ("toutes les évidence lui sont mystère", E, 14); questioning reaffirms its immense worth alongside new recognitions; vision can be polemical or political, but may be discreet though unbounded; the ethical, moral, spiritual dimension of all discourse is beyond mistake. Eighthly, as I have hinted above, language is always, in one way or another, at the centre of debate--"dès les premiers mots un voile recouvre le monde", Anne Teyssiéras characteristically and suggestively writes (CM, 66)--and thus obliquely, but most richly, such poetry feeds into much socio-political and philosophical analysis, feminist or other, of our time. As my ninth point, I should recommend remaining alert to what these poets commonly deem to be the unvoiced, the occulted, "la source de vie", as Céline Zins says, "[qui] est toujours souterraine" (AG, 120). A whole logic develops around such factors, inevitably linked to questions of language and expression, but perhaps even more importantly steeped in the sensation and perception of a self-discovery of infinite proportions: "Nous sommes", declares Heather Dohollau, "les hiéroglyphes de la profondeur/ Dans la profondeur même" (ML, (60)). Tenthly, it will not be unimportant to register and contemplate a whole cluster of elements centred around a rethought, though I should say equally instinctive, poetics of honour, courage, willingness to tackle issues either microscopic or macroscopic, viscerally felt or mentally caressed at some greater remove. Lastly--on this most provisional and manifestly incomplete list--there are many chiasmic points to be mapped out from poet to poet that would privilege notions-- lived, felt notions, it is important to stress--of becoming and transformation perceived *both* as passingness, ephemerality, *and* as a space-time of ever-new "belief"--"il est temps de croire", Andrée Chedid provocatively yet simply writes (TP, 159)--, of "burning and lasting advance" (Janine Mitaud: SB, 20), of ever-feasible self-assumption and self-rewriting. The slippage of life in this way contains its own transcendence, always unfoldable in the eternity of the *hic et nunc.*

Toulon and Halifax, 1994.

ANDRÉE CHEDID

Textes pour une figure (1949) is the first volume of poetry to be published by an author who will not only become France's most vigorous, accessible and widely read woman poet of the past forty years, but give herself generously to the realms of the theatre, the novel and the short story. The clarity of idea and emotion marking this early collection already demonstrates, as does its mode of orchestration, a constancy, an unclutteredness and a simple, natural passion that will not desert Andrée Chedid's subsequent writing, no matter what its generic orientation. The liminal poem, "Paysages" (TP, 17-19), manifests the attraction of the concrete, of what Bonnefoy terms "les choses du simple", and other texts reveal a fascinated sense of the events and dramas within which sand and sun, birds and water, trees and mountains unfold their destiny, a sense linking Chedid's work from the outset to the great tradition of Lamartine and Desbordes-Valmore, Vigny and Hugo. This tradition, moreover, is, again as with Chedid, by no means one of unemotional description, always opting for meditation and philosophico-psychological reflection over the dry rigours of strict externality. The very title of the volume, echoed by many to come, would seem to insist upon a purpose of language beyond direct portrayal, though the *figure* evoked, whilst one of words, should not be read as conferring upon her work a finicky aestheticism: if there is a desire to go beyond the real in Chedid, it is only ever in order to contemplate the face, the structure, of its profounder meaning. Thus is it that the physical, the mythical and the metaphysical ceaselessly intertwine in *Textes pour une figure* and that these early, but sure-footed texts may be read in easy harmony with the recent work of *Poèmes pour un texte (1970-1991)* or *7 are Plantes pour un herbier* (1985). Factors of human time are nuanced by Chedid's intuitions of vaster rhythms and cosmic scales; life and death enjoy paradoxical relations; love's problematics and the tensions of desire insert themselves into the physical in utterly natural but mysterious ways; the emotion of revolt rises up, fragile and improbable, in the face of the dire enigmas of violence and war, loss and anxiety. "Arlequin" (TP, 32) shows in high metaphoric mode a good deal of this, conjuring up in rapid succession images of solitude, nakedness, battle, rancour, fear, hunger, weeping and dried blood, all of which constitute the multiple "colours" of "ma robe d'Arlequin" the poet is offering herself. The poem ends as follows:

> Et je me suis coiffé du Blanc des faces mortes
> Pour danser devant Dieu
> Et distraire son regard de l'éternel ennui.

Rising above its own ironies, "Arlequin" succeeds in weaving a patchwork quilt of the real, at once acerbic and indicative of the resistant, transformational power of the creative imagination. "L'oeil dans l'oeil de la mort", as Chedid writes in "Révolte" (TP, 36), manages to maintain lucidness, yet it is too the means of our self-redefinition, an "otherness" that can re-tell "our history" (TP, 37). "Les Filles du vent" (TP, 40), the closing text of the collection, not dissimilarly speaks of a (feminine) parting, exile and uncertainty, yet generates recuperation where none seems available, remaining, presence and just feasible joy, where absence, anxiety and a sad knowing seem sure to prevail:

> Amies-soleil des tristesses
> Compagnes inquiètes de la joie
>
> Elles sont parties les filles qui savent
> Légères et lourdes
> De la chanson des mondes
> Elles sont parties
> Et elles sont là.

Chedid's next collection, *Textes pour un poème* (1950), will provide the title for the 1987 collective edition regrouping her poetic production up until 1970. Not only does its continuing relevance thereby appear demonstrated, but, echoing *Textes pour une figure* and other titles to follow shortly, it suggests a gathering, an ongoing effort, an offering of (mere, provisional, never perfectible) texts "for" some imaginable, ever-ideal poem still to come. Poetic form remains stable though open: unrhymed free verse, preferred stanza length of one to four lines, syllable-count per line varying from one to fourteen, with a predilection for the 5-8 syllable line. Syntax remains coherent, unelliptical, and various forms of rhythmic accumulation or quasi-repetition abound. Indentation rarely occurs in an effort of visual sculpting, as say in the early Reverdy. "Les Mouettes" (TP, 43) opens the volume and is a typical "structure", though bordering, as Chedid likes sometimes to do, upon the *chanson*, the *cantine* even, here. The poem, however, is always marked by intimacy, an immediacy of exchange, and, like other texts of the volume, quickly plunges us into a swirl of elements and intensely personally perceived experiences: "le goût des jardins sur les choses // La verte étoile d'un étang / Le rire bleu de la barque / ... / De l'aube entre les doigts / De l'ombre entre les tempes". A thematics of insufficiency and impotence is pursued, always in flashes and bursts, but it is outweighed and outmanoeuvred by the poet's insistence upon active response to cosmic and telluric appeal, upon the sheer power of her poetic "going", the "indocility" of her action before the trim "exactness" reality may seem to display (TP, 48, "Le Sel"). Although thus feeling her "strangeness"--she is newly transplanted from her native Cairo--she turns it to good account via memory, observation and, above all, that exploitation of all strangeness, of self and of other, that is creation, imagination. "Que les

19

sources sont étrangères", she exclaims in "Les Digues" (TP, 49-50), where she articulates well her confidence both in a sensed "harvesting" to come and in a bizarre rightness of the world's strangely frustrating unfolding. "Le Grain" (TP, 60-61) closes the volume and demonstrates in broad terms Chedid's earlier expressed need to generate a logic of the "heart"--depth, presence, feeling--as opposed to one of "fetish"--image, surface, idolatry (TP, 59). It is a poem of difficult accomplishment and self-renewal, a poem showing the full range of emotion experiencable within transformation and self-reidentification. As such it can traverse phases of surging clarity:

> C'est le moment où les enfants me reconnaissent
> Les terres sont prodigues comme des paraboles
> Le fruit tombe aux mains du vagabond;

yet its closing quatrain is paradoxical and enigmatic, speaking of "la mort systématique / Qui me brise d'une fissure / Propre comme un épi", and points to the complexities of an imagination and a psychology we never should take for granted.

By 1957 Andrée Chedid will have published four more collections of poetry, all with G.L.M., and will already have established herself, with *Le Sommeil délivré* (1952) and *Jonathan* (1955), as a writer of power, urgency and consistency. *Textes pour le vivant* (1953) is a book of commemoration and vision written upon the death of Chedid's father. It does not hesitate to invite us to rethink the equations of being and non-being, seeing our deeper mystery as "loin des ruelles exactes" (TP, 72), our reality as variable in form and state, slipping in and out of "other dimensions". Language, too, is necessarily buoyed up by some principle of "fidelity" and, under the sign of D. H. Lawrence, it is seen as an agent, a companion propagator, of life, "ce fruit d'espérance" (TP, 79).

The experience of presence Chedid traverses is certainly one of high sensory and sensual specificity, but it is equally inhabited by an "otherness" language faithfully, metaphorically, endeavours to evoke. The collection's long final four-part poem, "Seconde vie Icare" (TP, 83-8), thus may resort to characteristic dialectical-synthetical images, but its fundamental mode is one of intimately clairvoyant, telepathic and visionary clarity. It is thus surprisingly unesoteric, though speaking of exquisite ontic exchange, interpenetration, mosaic mysteriousness. "Toi qui sais que tout est autre chose encore"; "Aller aller toujours / où toutes vies se mêlent / Rêve et sang ne feront qu'un"; "La mort la facile mort cette lampe multipliée!" (TP, 84, 88)... *Textes pour la terre aimée* (1955), following two years later, reaffirms Chedid's essential focus: the *hic et nunc*, the experience and love of the earth now, despite our protests, our pain, our "ignorance". Such a reaffirmation links Chedid's poetics to that of poets such as Heather Dohollau, Janine Mitaud and Denise Le Dantec, and demonstrates larger contemporary affinities: Bonnefoy, Char and Jaccottet, in particular. The embrace of the contents of our passingness, our mortality, places us half-way between a questioning and a non-definitive answering, a desire to seize, somehow, "Les saisons de passage" (TP, 95) and a knowledge that our deeper meaning is caught up in this movement, this constant origination and unfinishedness, and that the latter, like dream's reality, frees, opens, renders all as "innocent" as a tree (TP, 92). "Il n'y a pas d'épilogue", the title of the volume's final text, is a recurring theme in Chedid's work (TP, 116). "Salut au poète" (TP, 107-8), moreover, offers a telling premonitory reminder of the vulnerability of poetry, indeed, implicitly, of all "strange" or "marginal" discourse wishing to remain free enough to "chante[r] la naissance téméraire de la rose d'azur / Cette jamais rencontrée". To the audacity

21

and liberation of the "le fruit essentiel" the poet calls forth, Chedid opposes the "écriture de pierre", the rigidity and oblivion that block the power of linguistico-existential self-transformation in our modern urban cultures.

Terre et poésie (1956) and *Terre regardée* (1957) explore in quite different modes the relationships Chedid perceives to be existing between our place of living, of being, and our manner of writing this place and these relationships. The first volume arguably shows the influence of Char--one thinks of *Fureur et mystère*--in its resorting to prose aphorisms assimilated to the poetic mode. Poetry is thus defined and redefined in its multiple pertinence: not given to renunciation (:we have already seen Chedid speak of its "fidelity"), it is intersectional rather than reconciliatory; it eschews circumscription and thus is precarious, though it does "force"; it is "naked", self-exposing, free, and, far from being a mere juggling of words, thus remains contemplative, openly attentive, equivalent to an act of love, a social intervention rearticulating social discourse, "[les poètes] assum[a]nt leur siècle, ses responsabilités; mais non ses formules" (TP, 129), in a true *acte de présence*. Although Chedid sees the danger of poetry being swamped by event, she understands too that its "breath" can and must "participate in the entirety of life" (TP, 135), repossibilising it and, as "naturally" and "suggestively" as life itself (TP, 130, 122), consenting to the role of the other in (self-)creation, in *poiesis... Terre regardée* pursues these preoccupations, reverting to the poet's established though somewhat expanding free verse forms. The 2-, 3- and 4-line stanzas dominate and an analysis of the stanzaic structure of the first five of the collection's twenty-nine poems reveals both stability and variety: 6+5+2(x5); 3+4; 2(x11) + 1; 5+2; 4x4. Only three stanzas in the entire volume exceed the 5-line length: 7, 8 and 11, the

22

latter constituting the full text of "L'Adolescent sans avenir" (TP, 168). Line length shows a marked tendency to increase: the alexandrine or its marginal 13-, 14-, 15-syllable extensions are common and the longer *verset* favoured by Claudel and Perse can occasionally be put to good effect, as in "Terre aimée" (TP, 159). New features emerge in the overall poetics: the Bonnefidian distinction between "image" and innocence; the somewhat Baudelairian relationship between beauty and attention ("Et toute chose fut belle d'avoir été chérie", TP, 149); a greater defiance of the earth's problems in the fervour of the poet's confident gaze ("Qu'elle gronde la menace... grand soleil perdu", TP, 159); the parallel conviction that life thrives upon "l'amour de vivre" (TP, 162), an again rather Bonnefidian will for being. "Terre des soifs" stresses, however, the replacement of simplicity by anguish that can afflict our collective consciousness, and other poems make clear that Chedid's thinking is not at all ungroundedly pollyanna-like: envy, crime, absurdity, destruction exist. "La Fleur d'orage" (TP, 173) persists however in arguing that "chaque fleur d'orage porte la graine de demain", just as "La Fleur du pèlerin" (TP, 179), which ends the collection, makes manifest Chedid's durability in the face of adversity, no doubt buoyed up once more by her dogged feeling that "une allée me prolonge / Loin du mortel pays", as she puts it in "L'Eau perpétuelle" (TP, 175).

Three volumes of poetry appear in the 1960's: *Seul, le visage* (1960), of similar compact length, *Double-pays* (1965), a short collection of some thirteen poems, and *Contre-chant* (1969), a decidedly more substantial book and Chedid's first poetic publication with Flammarion. "Double-pays" (TP, 183) opening the first of these three collections and anticipating the second, is as metaphorically rich and exquisite as any poem of Char's:

> Nous sommes faits
> Pour la mer sans fissure
> Pour le cygne incendié
> Pour notre double de la tour
> Pour la grappe d'une seule pluie
> Pour la falaise libre.

It, like other poems to follow, dwells upon the critical role of the heart, of feeling, of love, in our efforts of self-"repatriation", the idea that we pathologically--but reversibly--reject what most we cherish (TP, 185): reversibly, because the self is seen as always "in its own hands", because in turn ever "surviving" them (TP, 186). To "reconnaître en chacun le gisant superbe / Qui outrepasse les tombes et confond nos mémoires" (TP, 189) is not simply to perceive our extraordinary ontology, but to realise that the latter is a logic of extra-individuality, of constantly criss-crossing otherness, in which "les ténèbres de l'autre sont nos propres ténèbres" (TP, 185). The "strangeness" of our going, "entre le gris et l'étincelle" (TP, 187), is such as to make us, with Chedid, repeatedly question our meaning, our purpose and our identity. No wonder that she can declare, in "Cendres vives" (TP, 195), that our existence is "fabulous", fabled, essentially mythical or fictional, a movement angled back towards "le pays des toujours", away from the "inert paths" we have sluggishly generated for our provisionality. "Tels que nous sommes" (TP, 196) captures succinctly some of this thinking:

> Avant que l'univers ne nous habite,
> Nous habitions l'univers.
> ....
> Entre l'instant vécu et l'instant à vivre,
> S'inscrit notre visage éternel.

Thus does our being seem an "eternal" projection of the complex, free consciousness of our possibility; thus is the "face" that so often haunts Chedid one of a presence of infinite layering, endlessly moving palimpsests. "En quel lieu est la vie?", "Le Poème final" asks, now more understandably (TP, 199), and the implicit answer--everywhere--clarifies Chedid's seemingly anti-Mallarméan "Je ne crois plus aux naufrages" (TP, 203), for the act of "singing the triumphant face" (TP, 204) skips over the temptations of irony just as it avoids the deformations of sheer "play / ... / Betraying man who is nothing finite" (TP, 209). "Seul le visage est notre royaume, / Son jour traverse nos nuits", Chedid asserts at the close of the volume (TP, 210): its conceivable triumph is sufficient answer to the questions opening the same poem, "Seul, le visage", with its images of loss, dying, absence and utter uncertainty as to the very reason for writing.

Double-pays picks up, again in Charian fashion, upon the contradictoriness *and* the "sovereignty" of our traversal of existence. Questions of "combat" and "conflict" and the interrogation of the self's multiple identity are the order of the day. Self-universe interconnectedness is emphasised, as are its sub-forms such as the relationship between body and psychology, self and other. "Parfois l'accord" (TP, 215) explores such fascinations:

> J'habite chaque visage
> Les paumes de la vie se desserrent
> Je quitte mes traces
> ....
> J'enfonce dans les prunelles du monde
> L'accord est bref comme l'écho.

At such moments, the penetrating gaze we have seen stressed, say, in *Terre regardée* becomes *voyance*, psychical exchange, a brief, harmonious illumination of the oneness of the universe Chedid evokes from a different angle a few poems on:

> Le temps d'un intervalle
> Herbes et pierre sont une   (TP, 219).

25

"Le Fruit provisoire" (TP, 223) seems to answer obliquely, ever-metaphorically--this is poetic truth and authenticity: a constant swirl of changing analogies--the question she asks herself in "Hommes parmi les pierres" (TP, 221): "A quoi ressemblons-nous / Braises sur l'andoise des âges / ... / sentinelles sans réponse / Magiciens du cri?" We are self-interpreters, self-interrogators, plunged into our symbols, our metaphoric self-definitions, our mere (*but infinite*) likenesses, "paroles interprétant nos brumes / Interrogeant nos déserts". And, above all, we are not essentially physical (as the closing poem, "Je t'aime, hostile oiseau", (TP, 225-6) affirms); rather are we creatures of imagination, constantly reseeding the soil of our being, creating provisional flowering even in the midst of all that works against it:

> Partout la graine imagine
> Et le printemps s'accorde à ce qui le détruit
>
> Partout se recompose le fruit provisoire
> La fleur sans détours habite parmi les bruits.

1968 is the telling date of publication of the aptly titled *Contre-Chant*. The volume offers, however, neither politicised discourse nor the kind of *contre-chant* or *mécriture* that have tempted Denis Roche and Bernard Noël. Chedid's main concern is to articulate forcefully her particular sense of what she calls, in the poem so titled, "Ce nous en nous" (TP, 249): our profound otherness, our teeming options, all seen in emotional, mythical and metaphysical terms, though deeply rooted in our experience of the earth. (We could, of course, think of other "revolutionary" writers in feasible relation to Chedid, and intertextual traces could readily be adduced: Rimbaud; Tzara; the surrealists, especially Eluard and Breton; Reverdy, Char, Michaux, but also various feminist writers, Colette, Weil, De Beauvoir...) Chedid's *contre-chant* is

26

not, in short, desperate, grating anti-writing, but an endeavour to have poetic language "shareable", *singingly* active *against* the "supplices. Hécatombes. / Nasses du malheur. Phénix de la haine" that can proliferate ("Contre-chant", TP, 234). Her *contre-chant* thus would reinvent ideality, the simplicity of some "oiseau irrécusable" (TP, 242); it would restore to our deserts "des fêtes d'herbe", care and cultivation to "nos champs illimités [en friche]" (TP, 277, 281). The very negative definitions (and consequent roles and acts) within which we have confined ourselves need thus--seemingly paradoxically, for they seem but to follow reality--to be freed up, transmuted. "Avant" (TP, 256) underscores this improbable possibility of self-recreation, -redescription, -reprojection:

> C'est avant ta naissance que se hasarde ta vie
> C'est avant ton regard que résident tes images.

Via such constant "escape / From what says [us]" (TP, 289), Chedid hopes to accede to what *Contre-Chant*'s final poem calls our "Visage intarissable", "visage le plus nu" (TP, 290): a counter-being of stark simplicity, of infinite difference within unity.

The 1970's see the publication of three major collections of poetry that we shall have occasion to deal with here: *Visage premier* (1972), *Fraternité de la parole* (1976) and *Cavernes et soleils* (1979). Other volumes appearing are *Fêtes et lubies* (1973) and *Cérémonial de la violence* (1976). *Visage premier* constitutes a blatant, passionate though lucid celebration of the "face" of being via all things and persons. It is for this reason perhaps that Chedid will argue in her liminal text the extent to which poetry is a place of joining, within the self, though for all, and even if no reconciliation of tensions seems practically and immediately available. In this sense poetry, as for a Frénaud, offers "evidence" and "suspension" simultaneously: freshness, fiery creativity and overflowing

27

fertileness to override those Baudelairian "wounds", dislocation and unfinishedness. Chedid's, and poetry's, consciousness would thus be "axial" (PT, 20), able to absorb dialectical perception, paradox, reversal-- the *puis, pourtant* abound in this poetry. The "goingness" Chedid so commonly sees herself as caught up in (PT, 26) can thus be viewed as a turning, a cyclical, circular movement, as endless and infinitely spacious in its experience as are the anaphoras, metaphors, shifting cumulative rhythms of her expressive mode itself. "*Vivre* innove le logis", she writes (PT, 29): living and creating ceaselessly, though mortally, turn and turn within the infinitely renewed sphere of their dovetailed function. Thus is it, in "Après le jardin" (PT, 31), that opening, nudity and alterity are preferred to the repose and purely edenic quality of the original garden. "Plus loin   plus loin que nous", Chedid writes in "Des soleils encore verts" (PT, 39), "Forgés d'autres mythes / Se hisseront des soleils / A face insoupçonnée!" Our imagination, our emotions, our thinking: all must be fluvial, moving, able to perceive the nearness within our difference, the gentleness of "toutes nos clairières inavouées" available beyond our fears (PT, 49). "Eveille en toi l'autre regard", Chedid prompts us, and herself, not for the first time (PT, 51), stressing once more, in "L'Echange" (PT, 52), along with other recognisable preoccupations, her improbable but profoundly significant sense of a cosmic unity and interconnectedness that transcends arguments of existential ignorance and banal chance:

> Inachevé pourtant
> Je vais et puis je vais
> Vers des régions toujours à naître
>
> Mais que je suis
> Mais que je sais.

"Pour renaître" (PT, 65) is the fourth text of *Fraternité de la parole* and approaches similar questions from a different angle. "Ils

28

meurent nos vieux soleils", it begins, "Ils meurent pour mieux renaître //
Astres d'une seule récolte / qui fourmillent d'infini". A confidence
persists, in all cosmic life forms, that enables a deft transcendence of
anguishing specificity and the embrace of our--everything's--vast,
unlimited renascent powers. Against such an ever-repossibilised
"backcloth", our odd contradictions play themselves out as simultaneously
absolute and relative: "Nous jouons l'existence / Contre un décor / qui
fuit". "Selon notre regard" (PT, 77-8) is a poem that develops such a
thematics of relativity, once more differently. It dwells, on the one hand,
upon the psychological, temperamental--and implicitly chosen, choosable--
structure of our perception of the real, according to which the *same*
phenomena, for different individuals and gazes, "rabattent leurs portes de
plomb / Ou s'avivent de clartés"; on the other hand, the poem ponders the
very genetic and behaviouristic development of such a structure of
endlessly differentiated perception. A later poem, "Percé de lucarnes"
(PT, 90), merits quoting in its compact but telling entirety:

> Débusque ce *battement-de-nous*
> gravé dans l'énigme
>
> Explore cette *trame-de-nous*
> où l'univers s'avive
>
> Le coeur percé de lucarnes
> Reconnais la rencontre
>
> Sacre l'éphémère.

Enigma may thus arguably prevail, but we are part of it, a vital vibration
or existential rhythm dwelling within it. The imperatives give, moreover,
to enigma an urgent psychological value, an intrinsic meaning, not
surprisingly in a poet insisting upon the interconnection of eternal mystery
and actuality, universal function and individually woven structure. The
heart, as always, remains the key, the window upon (self-)recognition, the

means of restoring to the fleeting its sacred, atemporal meaning. Many other factors deserve our critical attention in *Fraternité de la parole*. Let me mention merely Chedid's emphasis, in her liminal text, upon the unifying and exalting function of poetic speech, through "ailes et chutes, enlisements et flambées" and despite "nos enclos, nos Babels, nos ravages" (PT, 61); her view, like that of many contemporary feminists, that our bodies are the locus of "so much unknownness", a material place so rich psychologically, spiritually if you like; the importance, finally, of the collection's last long poem, "Le Feu du dedans" (PT, 98-102), with its endless urgings, its logics of externality and internality, its poetics of self-expression, translation and silence, and, above all perhaps, its psychology of celebration, "singing" and *salut* (:greeting and salvation).

Like so many of Chedid's volumes, the 1979 *Cavernes et soleils* is warmly dedicated to a friend, even in the 1991 collective edition, *Poèmes pour un texte (1970-1991)*. Generally shorter line structure is favoured here and, indeed, in all the work to come afterwards. The 6-, 7- or 8-syllable line dominates, but shorter metric structures are quite common, whereas the alexandrine or the longer *versets* are quite rare. Stanzaic preferences remain much as they were, at once varied, freely patterned, yet guided by principles of darting brevity, and thus 2-, 3-, 4- and 5-line structures. Prose elements are smoothly and unqueryingly inserted into the volume, and a few longer poems have more prominent roles than usually has been the case--even here, however, there is a tendency to divide the poem into sections, either numbered or anaphorically and typographically rhythmed: "Sommeil contradictoire" (PT, 145-54) and "Prendre corps" (PT, 157-77) are good examples. Great imaginative and ideational richness continues, as Chedid stresses from the outset: "Pas de terme au mystère des choses naturelles: l'ailleurs est ici"

(PT, 105). Existence is thus for her unfathomable but buoying "effervescence". She develops in particular the metaphor of "grafting" both poetically and in her prose text "Chantier du poème" (PT, 115-18): each *greffe*, for better or for worse, represents an act of (self-)creation, modification, renewal, *poiesis*. (One can read each of Chedid's poems as line-by-line, stanza-by-stanza, grafts, healing, generating, cross-breeding, infinitely creative measures of being.) The volume's poetics, as elsewhere, can veer to the tormented--"L'aube est moribonde / Boues et supplices surnagent / Les credos ont pourri", we read in Sèves et déchets" (PT, 120)--but as this poem's very title shows, Chedid's powers of imaginative recuperation and equilibration are unflagging: our cosmic *sèves*, our *soleils*, risk winning out over our *déchets*, our ontic self-pollution, our dank *cavernes*. "Si Dieu est / Il ne sait point se dire", Chedid can, perhaps surprisingly, maintain, though beyond dogmatic appropriation. The "divine", have we not seen already, ultimately depends upon *our* individual and collective capacity to consecrate the ephemeral? If the consciousness of death is strong in a number of poems, freedom's "stubborn genesis", though requiring vigilance, is not really doubted. Once more, I can only invite the reader to meditate the beauty and the pertinence of the volume's last two long poems, "Sommeil contradictoire" and "Prendre corps".

The poetry of the 1980's is principally marked by the publication, in 1983, of *Epreuves du vivant*. A good deal of other shorter work has appeared in reviews, and been finally published in book form in the 1991 *Poèmes pour un texte*--and I shall look at this in conclusion--but *Epreuves du vivant* remains Chedid's major recent poetic collection of the period. There are, moreover, arguable links between the volume and the earlier poems of *Cérémonial de la violence* (1976)--which Chedid nevertheless

31

elects to omit from the 1991 edition, its "tonality" felt to be somewhat overly specific, insufficiently "enraciné[e] à une terre commune et de tous lieux" (PT, 187)--to the extent that existential difficulty and trial predominate imaginatively. "Epreuves en noir et en or" (PT, 187) thus demonstrates the polarisation of individual experience:

> Au loin
> Sous l'explosion des armes
> Les terres ne cessent de gémir
> ....
> Ici
> Enlacé d'ombres vertes
> Et de fêtes

and we realise quickly that the anguish felt can stem not only directly from the violences of Lebanon and the Middle East and indeed so many other parts of our planet, but also, contradictorily, from a sense of our own ease and peace, pleasure and simplicity. Chedid's wisdom, however, resides in not falling into the trap either of personal guilt or of specific recrimination: rather does she prefer symbols of illumination and redemption: "Ces lucarnes trouant l'opaque / Ces lunes rachetant l'obscur // Je mise sur ces clartés / Profondes et périssables" (PT, 193). Only such symbols, elementary but intense, seem able to brighten our dullness, lovingly heal our modern, Baudelairian *fêlures*, pacify our ontic "base", see--again like a Baudelaire or the Tournier of *Petites proses*--beauty in "le squame des malheurs" (PT, 193, 196, 199). The Michaux-like Tree of Life may then, via such chosen symbolic, metaphoric perception, "m'élance[r] hors des décombres / Vers la parole-fruit" (PT, 222). The short prose texts, "Epreuves de l'écrit" and "Epreuves du titre" (PT, 200-204, 205-6), stress however that symbolic, linguistic inscription is nevertheless very much caught up in the dialectical pull of the raw existential trial the poet lives: it is not a simple, readily transcendent act;

its success--its very possibility--depends upon a constant reimmersion in natural mystery and a subsequent effort of expressive production that is always incomplete, vulnerable, "testing". Such an effort, however, is "notre chance", our "risk" of existential transmutation. Chedid explains furthermore that her preference for the volume's chosen title, over that of one of its key poems, "La Table des poussières" (PT, 207-8), represents a critical choice of overall symbolic value: whilst the latter poem's title would have risked placing the volume under the sign of some dusty, desertic burial of the present, "Epreuves du vivant" bears the signature of "le faire, le défaire, le refaire, mouvements de la vie même, qui m'importent!" Chedid's feeling that the individual's journey, like the collectivity's, is an inner one, spiritual and psychological though projected into the symbols of physicality, restores buoyancy to her sense of our inimitable, extravagant *parcours*, of which the poem is but a moving trace. The collection's closing text, "La Vie voyage" (PT, 225-6) captures much of this.

"Tant de corps et tant d'âme" gives its title to the various clusters of poems Chedid offers us in her 1991 collective edition as representative of her work after *Epreuve du vivant*, and it is also the title of the liminal text of this selection, divided further into five groupings: our liminal text and "Au fond du visage"; *Les Rythmes du temps*; *7 textes pour un chant*; *L'Énigme-Poésie*; and *Chemins à vivre*. "Tant de corps et tant d'âme" (PT, 229-33) is a longer, tripartite poem centred upon an interrogation of being perceived not only as lived actuality but as organising principle, "qui prononce notre mort / Qui instaure notre vie". Terms such as *présence* and *absence, vallées* and *gouffres, rixes* and *roses* are but--as is each line/poem in Chedid's poetics--provisional metaphors for seemingly separate aspects of such being. Globally, the poet sees a liberating--

probably reintegrating--movement going from "l'arbre de chair / Vers les récits du monde / Vers l'image inventée": such fictions are, in all likelihood, not just our earthly poems and mental structures, but vaster cosmic images and projections "explaining" the latter constantly "débauchant l'espérance". "Le Temps-tisserand" (PT, 236), from *Les Rythmes du temps*, I would mention briefly for two reasons: its still eminently characteristic use of anaphoric and cumulative structures, allied to its non-elliptical grammar and its liking for global semantic coherence and thus carefully rounded poetic closure; secondly, the interwoven ideas of mortality, extratemporal reawakening and oblivion, here wrapped in somewhat atypical uncertainty, the poem being more philosophic than urgently personal. "La Vérité" (PT, 259), from *Chemins à vivre*, provides a powerful indictment of fanaticism and narrowly focussed vision: truth overdetermined, Chedid rightly argues, becomes a lie, a mirage; it congeals, limits, divides and opposes. Rather, she claims, does truth sow abundant seed for an infinite harvest. "Saluons", she writes in the closing stanza:

> Saluons plutôt nos soleils transitoires
> Nos paroles libres d'emblème
> Nos chemins en chemin
> Nos multiples horizons.

Truth as openness, plurality, developing vision, unattached to hardened emblem, a mere movingness of our being in all its strange and contorted aspirations and desires. The *7 Textes pour un chant* offer seven--a recurrent figure in Chedid--poems that, whilst accomplishing, according to the logic of "La Vérité", provisional gestures of high aspiration, realise that their collective power, whilst "lacking / *The* Song", nevertheless moves us in some measure towards an undreamed meaning, "vers *l'autre* sens", as "Trajectoires du chant" (PT, 248) puts it. No absolute attainment, no absolute truth, may thus be feasible in Chedid's poetics; but, as the seventh *texte* suggests, such transitoriness, such mere poetic "going" remains fragilely attached to The Song:

> Nourri de chants
> Le Chant
>
>> Etend la parole
>> Traverse âges et murailles
>
> Eveille d'autres chants
>
>> Ensemence.   (PT, 249)

This is no small gesture, and no small understanding of the meaning and function of poetry.

HEATHER DOHOLLAU

Although a younger Heather Dohollau wrote a number of poems in English, it was not until many years after leaving her native South Wales to settle in Western France's wild and exotic Ile de Bréhat that her first work in French was published. *Seule enfance* (1978) is a slender volume, but its twenty-seven texts possess already that delicacy, that serenity and that grace which unfailingly mark all the work to come, from *La Venelle des portes* and *La Réponse* to *L'Adret du jour* and *Les Portes d'en bas*. Its overall poetics, too, demonstrates that Dohollau, whilst fascinated by the multiplicity of phenomena and our experience of them, remains a writer of high, and long-meditated, consistency. The opening poem, part one of twelve independent reflections upon time, its passingness and its dimensions exceeding such passingness, begins as follows:

> Regardons maintenant de face:
> D'où part le cri
> Quel est le tir, la cible   (SE, 1).

A poetics of looking, lucidly yet contemplatively, is thus quickly established, and we understand that the "cry" and the "arrows" afterwards evoked reveal a concern with the logistics of being: its origin, its directionality, its intentionality. The poems that follow, compact in stanzaic and metric pattern, plunge us, with that odd calmness that haunts Dohollau's work, into dizzying knots of temporal inquiry, questions of presence and absence--"chaque pas a[yant] son poids / De néant" (SE, 3)--, dream and reality: "Tu faisais déjeuner / L'invisible / Faute de réel" (SE, 4). One of the dominant elements of her poetics, namely the essential impossibility of ontic loss regardless of physical occurrence, also affirms

36

itself in this initial suite of texts: "Là, où il n'y a pas de route / Qui peut se perdre?", she asks, and far, it should be stressed, from the conflicts and ironies of Frénaud's *Nul ne s'égare*; still further from the thematics of general exile characterising the yet meticulously vigorous quest of, say, Jabès. Indeed, this poetics of non-loss, non-losableness, is, whilst not sociologically characterised, eminently feminine and feminist: despite all-- Chedid and Hyvrard have together said enough--, spiritual and psych(olog)ical (re)affirmation is quietly rampant. Dohollau's *Seule enfance* already shows, in tentative, not fully blossomed, mode, both the recognition of earthly forms of beauty and the role of dream, "transcendent" reality and the *imaginaire*--and suggests what will come more persistently later: their interpenetration, perhaps their very equivalence. Varyingly lived presences can thus be deemed angelic, and, just as time's dimensions seem mysteriously interconnected, so can space appear harmonious, unified, "ici et là se balança[nt] doucement" (SE, 10). The beautiful prose poem, "Il y a un monde..." (SE, 15), reveals similar preoccupations, subtly evoked rather than argued, manifestly resting upon experience at once sensual and spiritual yet not urgent with any need to convince:

> Il y a un monde créé par le souffle des sensations, de parfums et de lueurs trouvés au bout de longs couloirs raccourcis dans l'instant.
>
> Un monde où nous nous éveillons autres en nous-mêmes, la certitude d'un rêve arraché colorant encore nos yeux de jour.
>
> Un pays sans profondeur où les choses déversent sur nous comme des vagues, nous laissant un corps d'écume.

Ce sont les oiseaux qui gardent l'accès, le ciel est un bruit
d'ailes, la terre, un pied nu dans l'herbe. Nous connaissons
le proche d'un lointain infini.

A micro-world within terrestrial existence; experience compacted into
some magical but simple now; the otherness of our presumed selfhood,
the fusable dimensions of our being; the Bonnefidian "frothiness" of our
physicality, exquisite yet far from our full profundity; our merging of the
frameworks of finitude and infiniteness....

"Des choses si simples" (SE, 16) are at the root of the experiences
Dohollau's poetry conveys, and it is thus not surprising that Jaccottet and
Bonnefoy have expressed their admiration for her work. "A partir d'un
moment d'une extrême simplicité", she writes in "Hölderlin à la tour"
(SE, 17), "il ne faut plus espérer". No typical 20th-Century stoicism here,
no feeling that love and transparency will not suffice. "Monterchi" (SE,
18) articulates boldly yet without ambition the fragile near-ineffableness
of presence, the fructuation and truth of existence in spite of the
problematics of intellectualisation thrown up about it. Other poems speak
of the gift of contact and perception suddenly bestowed upon us, or of the
experienced sacredness of time's slippage, its link to "ideality" and
extratemporalness. Colours possess a mystery for Dohollau as for Du
Bouchet--and perhaps there are intertextual echoes here of Gautier,
Baudelaire and Rimbaud. Space-time becomes utterly relative, porous, and
life unfolds "dans un lieu de rien pour la poursuite de tout" (SE, 21). The
endless simple things of Dohollau's poetry are thus implacably bonded to
the limitless. "Une étroite bande d'herbe / Sert de passage / À l'illimité
/ Un tapis tendu / Pour les pieds de l'ange" (SE, 25), she declares in "Les
Jardins de la Giudecca". So felt is her language that she can

characteristically and tellingly ask in the seventh and final text of her "Point de Venise" (SE, 26):

Sommes-nous à l'extérieur
De nous-mêmes.

Her question remains unanswered, but it is clear from this poem of *Seule enfance* as of others to come that our exile from ourselves, incurring no loss, can only leave us in what she calls "les lieux fidèles / D'un paradis jamais perdu".

Two years later appears, with Folle Avoine who will perceptively continue to publish all her subsequent work, *La Venelle des portes* (1980). Like the volumes to come, it is a more fully developed collection. Formally, too, it takes much further the patterns of *Seule enfance*, whose stanzaic preferences tended to either the 5-, 6-, 7- or 8-line structure or to the 10-, 11-, 12-, 13-line verse, and whose line-length moves from short to longish (12, 13, even 15 syllables) and settles rather for medium syllabic rhythm. Three prose poems appear in *Seule enfance*, whereas *La Venelle des portes* has seven, the rest all, again, in unrhymed free verse. The volume's first poem, "Pour V. W." (VP, 1), sets the tone for this added freedom--11 unpunctuated lines, of widely varying length (8-18 syllables), yet almost all long: 13x3, 15, 16x2, 17, 18 -- yet it remains an aesthetically circumscribed freedom, visually and not just metrically, though this aestheticism, one feels, is generally visceral or unconscious with Dohollau, and certainly far from being a dominant factor. This is no doubt because Dohollau's essential focus is rather upon experience than upon questions of transcription or textual interiority and autonomy. Poetry, for her, is never an end, nor a dead end. It may cast the poet in the role of "funambule sur le fil des mots par-dessus les eaux irréelles", but it aims to explore self's relation to reality come what may. Reception of language's symbols and images is a notion Dohollau finds pertinent in Novalis: an open, half-lucid, half-trance-like (because entranced) scriptural posture is not a failure, then, but a mode of expression precisely corresponding to what she will call "le tremblé du vrai" (VP, 37), in "La Mer ce matin..."

Given, however, Dohollau's specifically ontological poetics, it is helpful to push a little further her still emerging sense of the real. Presence, for her, is a deep, layered and infinite *gestalt*. It is persistently regarded as "angelic", in sunlit gardens, along quiet paths, and so on. Physically manifested, it remains a psych(olog)ical, spiritual phenomenon, its "things" ever caught up in gentle emotion and barely describable soul experience. "De si peu de choses sont faits les paysages de l'âme", she notes (VP, 9): the mountains, the trees, the rain of such ephemeral epiphenomena, exquisitely constituting a reality "disguised as itself" (VP, 6) and at the very centre of the world in their hereness and nowness (VP, 11), go beyond their sheer physical grace and beauty in providing "le viatique et le voyage" (VP, 14) leading us back to the forgotten but not lost profundity of our being. To gaze upon things in simplicity, theirs *and* ours, is to surpass their "aestheticism": it invites our love of them, which in turn gives access to a beauty that is at once an ethics and a spirituality. Such a gaze or perception leaps beyond mere intellectualism, sees cosmic and divine meaning beyond dogma or system in, for example, a wintry scene "[qui] est la vitre de l'amandier en fleurs" (VP, 26), or the distant passage of "deux femmes [qui] parlent / Du temps, des enfants / Cousues dans le jour / Par les points invisibles de l'heure / Sur une route d'étoile" (VP, 30). Things in special places, Ravenna, Venice, etc., we might argue, as for Lamartine or Bonnefoy; but there remains even here--and most special places for Dohollau are of the heart first and foremost--an ordinariness, an anonymousness even, showing that the real magic is a "mandala de maintenant" (VP, 47) and that the most perceptive "seeing" always involves imaginative or dream-like, emotional or psychical "transcendence". "Ici comme partout", she affirms, "vivre c'est fermer les yeux" (VP, 53).

La Venelle des portes offers much else, of course, but its principal focus is telluric and metaphysical in a simple Donne-like mode, eschewing grand myths, relying upon the depth of meditated moments of considerable inconspicuousness. "Keeping the impossible intact" could be her motto (VP, 70) for much of the collection. And in pursuing this purpose, Dohollau does not forget that our path is infinite not just in the choices made, but in those not made: our ontic spaciousness is in effect much more vast than we tend to believe, above all in an optic wherein time and space erase their customary frontiers and truth "trembles" as in a haze of newly revealing feasibility. If anguish and consciousness of desert and the power of fear have their role to play in all of this, it serves to show that La Venelle des portes remains a rooted, unhermetic book of poetry. And if Constable and Balthus, as other painters will soon, insert themselves into Dohollau's poetics, it is no doubt because, firstly, her husband, Tanguy Dohollau, is an artist -- who has provided beautiful frontispieces for most of her collections; and, secondly, and partly in consequence, her work focusses persistently upon the relationship of self and world through seeing, and the logic of the latter.

Matière de lumière (1985) is the cornerstone work of Heather Dohollau: it confirms the exceptional delicacy of her poetic genius, is in itself a major collection of some hundred pages, and offers certain poems and fragments as fine-nerved and as memorable as any I know.

Comment perdre ce qui est toujours là
Le vrai incroyable
La présence d'un feu, un lit, un jardin
L'ombre en tête d'oiseau de la plume
N'est pas plus fidèle
Que ces lieux où nous vivons
Par la caution des choses

La table, les chaises, les fleurs
Dans l'eau des heures
L'espace partagé
Où en tendant la main
Nous poussons la porte du présent
Et le regard s'arrondit comme un fruit   (ML, 93).

Such a poem as this is above all a meditation upon our being, and in that it is no "joli méli-mélo" as Roche has said of a certain modern poetry, but rather serenely "combative", unpretentiously purposeful. Founded upon what Bonnefoy terms *confiance* and afffirmation of our pure provisionality, one could also relate Dohollau's *vrai incroyable* to symbolist aspiration if it were not for her sense of ideality being *already* available--perhaps Rimbaud comes very close, however, in certain texts, and, much nearer to us, with his particular but universal pertinency, does not Michel Deguy speak of the need to "ineffacer le devenu-incroyable"? Dohollau's own particularities nevertheless make the intertextual interest fade: the caressing of familiar, faithful, "banal" things, the implicit rendering secondary of the act of writing, the idea of time's watery unifiedness, the sharedness of existence, the sense of presence's fullness via our fortifying gaze--these are some of the particular signs of a consciousness as finely, self-effacingly articulated, "rounded out", as experience itself.

"Je te cherche" (ML, 32), an earlier and more compact poem, is even more fragile in its contemplative and structural qualities:

42

Je te cherche
Es-tu ma mère, ma fille?
Laquelle est la porte de l'autre
La terre est là
Au niveau de nos songes
Faut-il descendre et monter
Pour y être
À portée de tes bras?

The poem's lightness, its questioning yet serene buoyancy, its throw-away yet softly reflective quality--these are elements that remind one, in the broadest terms possible, of the work, especially *inédits* such as "Les Roses de Saadi", of the yet inimitable Marceline Desbordes-Valmore. The mother-daughter thematics is similarly evocative, though the questions raised about time and identity, the fusions that inhabit them, the openness of initial reference and the syntactic ambiguity of the second line--all these are factors characteristic of Dohollau, as are the image of the "door" of being (: birth, knowledge, recognition, revelation) and the linking of (physical) being-there and the reality of (day-)dream. The question upon which the poem ends does not, it should be noted, centre on the beauty and feasibility of contact, but rather upon the rhythmic means of mutual access, of love--beyond what we think of as love, in all probability. One of the untitled prose poems of *Matière de lumière* might be as it were apposed to this finishing, gently questioning meditation. It shows, moreover, similar tonal and emotional qualities:

> Ce vide au coeur de l'amour est une chose merveilleuse, il n'existe pas pour être comblé, c'est lui qui comble. Comme la musique aboutit au silence, tout tend vers cet instant où les mains tombent. Plus rien à donner, plus rien à prendre. Le monde est perçu en son origine, et le temps n'est qu'un rêve de l'espace.   (ML, 90)

The poem is rich in implication, though elegantly concise and uncluttered. Its poetics of love and desire as a void that nevertheless offers plenitude can be linked to Reverdy's and Char's writings on poetry, but here, as usual, Dohollau's focus remains primary being rather than aesthetic transmutation albeit with its ontological significance. The questions of "Je te cherche" disappear here, though both poems possess a strange calm and poise, a sure sense of the intricate network of the meaning of being, beyond time, beyond space, a meaning of original joinedness, of an affective state precisely beyond any real questioning. One of the closing poems of *Matière de lumière* may be cited to show the quiet tension between assurance and search, acceptance of mystery and anxious query:

Toujours nous cherchons une porte
Dans le jour
De cette terre

Un moyen
De rester
Au ciel où nous sommes   (ML, 99).

Matière de lumière continues to unfold the magic of its places: Pieve, Rome, Pavese; but there are also poems of Penarth, Cardiff, l'Ile de Bréhat, la rue Brizeux where the poet currently resides. And artistic inspiration or interpenetration develops still further: Rembrandt, Piero, Cézanne, Manet, Van Gogh, Morandi, with additional reference to Pound, Keats and Robin. The poem is viewed as a temporary dwelling, a shelter against oblivion, a "shadow" of life's brilliance. "Ecoutant l'éternel / parler de ses arbres" (ML, 38) is what really seduces Dohollau, though, if correspondingly she can say that "ici et maintenant est l'eau que l'on verse / Sur la tête d'un dieu" (ML, 44), the poem still stands as an emblem of such sacred primal acts. "Nous sommes les hiéroglyphes de la profondeur / Dans la profondeur même", she tranquilly writes of our complexity (ML, 60), understanding well, as few poets do, the extent to which "ce que nous ne sommes pas / Est ce que nous sommes" (ML, 61).

44

In a style of great delicacy and bare insistence, her poetic gesture seeks merely to "écri[re] ce que pour moi est mystère" (ML, 88), to unassumingly convey the essential part of her experience of "Ici [qui] parlait l'indicible" (ML, 84).

1989 sees the publication of two other substantial collections, *Pages aquarellées* in April, *L'Adret du jour* in June. The first of these volumes, written under the sign of Shakespeare--"out of this nettle, danger / we pluck this flower, safety"--with a further epigraph from the often torn, but here contemplative, Jouve dwelling upon some mysterious unity in the colouredness of the variegated earth--the first volume, then, could allow for a full-scale study of Dohollau's ekphrastic proclivities: poems "from" or "for" Constable, Turner, Klee, Morandi, Cézanne, Balthus, Jones, Moore and others. Largely gone are the Italian sites, replaced by places of Southern France, Switzerland and those blatant or implicit in the "Lumières du Nord" suite. Presence and reality continue to centre Dohollau's preoccupations. She insists upon factors of ephemeralness, the "melting snow" of being--an image Bonnefoy explores too in his later *Début et fin de la neige*; life's infinitesimal movements of "fidelity" and yet the opaqueness and invisibility of so much, perception's relativity, which makes such "fidelity" so precious; the movingness of things, which nevertheless accomplishes "le retour / Magique du même" (PA, 29); our ontic improbability (: "Nous sommes où nous sommes si peu", PA, 42), which explains Dohollau's feeling of her/our constant rebirth, our plunging into our otherness; and so on, the list of factors stretches on: death's life; the mute language of presence traversing materiality; the exquisite specificity of, say, fuchsia's colouredness, rejecting out of hand the absurd and unidimensional, chemical mortality; "the laughter [of things] shining / In the morning of the world" (PA, 63). Perhaps one of

45

the poems from "La Maison de la vie" conjures most aptly both
Dohollau's sense of existential fragility *and* certainty, and the fine, honest
transparency of her style:

Je cherchais le réel
Hors la fuite des heures
Les lieux du mirage
Mais ce fut le cercle
Instable du présent
Qui livrait le monde
Ce fruit de l'air   (PA, 47).

As many other poems confirm, Dohollau's point of anchorage remains the
now, shimmering, precarious, but livable, penetrable, offered like a
gateway into the full flavour of what and where we already are. All
"esotericism" thus folds back into an embrace of our simplicity--that yet
yields up an airy fullness, a ripe etherealness.... Poetry thus functions as
a means of access, a "window", upon the otherness we already are and
inhabit (PA, 43); and yet, whilst, also in "La Maison de la vie", Dohollau
can therefore maintain that "les mots dans l'épaisseur fleurissent plus
loin", she can dialectically-synthetically add that "leur graine retombe
dans l'espace du corps" (PA, 42), for language is equally visceral,
physical and its function is that of "guaranteeing things" (PA, 41),
articulating the "things" of experience rather than escaping into some
prison-house of Mallarméan interiority or some wild non-referentiality.
Metaphoricalness may be inevitable--"L'odeur d'une rose / Est vaste et
précise / *Comme* pour une mouette la mer", Dohollau writes in "Le Jardin
de Bréhat" for example (AP, 62)--but these "watercolour pages" orient our
attention without respite towards "les jours de pluie le poids du chat" (PA,
45): the signs of externality, caught up in--*as*--a reflection profound and
mysterious.

46

L'Adret du jour follows closely upon the appearance of *Pages aquarellées* and its title, insisting on the southerly, sun-lit time-space of existence, may be linked to the collection's next-to-closing page (thus providing a clear framing for the poems contained within), where Novalis' quoted words remain essential to our ontological purpose: "Le paradis est en quelque sorte dispersé sur la terre entière, diffusé partout--et c'est pourquoi il est devenu si méconnaissable. Ses traits épars doivent être réunis, son squelette réhabillé" (AD, 78). The volume's opening text, "Les pentes sont couvertes..." (AD, 5), from the section entitled "Le château d'en bas", revolves contemplatively around the simple, given things of the earth, hillsides, fir-trees, but, on the one hand, the latter are draped in fine metaphor--*laine de sapins, haleine des mousses*--and, on the other, the poem seeks to deal with the difficult spiritual challenge involving the elevation of perturbing existential perception and experience, "mémoires de meurtres et de rapts dans l'espace [..] vers les cimes dans la haute splendeur du vrai". Dohollau thus openly tackles the aporia of anguish in an effort to suggest that such "présences [restent] nues d'un vide frais de sens". The last of the three quatrains (each with a metric stability still allowing freedom: 13-13-12-15 syllables, 13-14-13-15, 14-15-13-15) reads as follows:

Les cheminements du souffle sont devenus les ponts
Suspendus entre les pierres et les bas-côtés de fleurs
Où les pas rédiment la perte d'un sol ancien
Et les yeux apportent à l'âme des seaux tremblants de bleu

Referentially and thus semantically fluid, these lines nevertheless confirm Dohollau's shift from the metaphors of shadow that beset "le château du coeur", to images of breath, no doubt both existential and poetic, that allow transfer, transmutation and redemption to occur via passsingness. The final image of implicit cooling of the soul by means of the gaze's

47

reimmersion in the azure evokes that earlier "freshening" of the void of existence by restoring meaning, and equally seems to reconcile matter and spirit, earlier threatened so dramatically.

A short look at three other poems from *L'Adret du jour* will have to suffice to capture some of the subtleties and insistences of a collection at times inspired by the art of Bonnard and Fragonard. "L'Amandier en fleurs" (AD, 27) could be compared with Jaccottet's "Le Cerisier" from the 1990 *Cahier de verdure*, even though the latter is much more extensive, in prose, and manifestly discursive in intention:

Un arbre si léger
Cette vie en dehors
Qui monte aux yeux
Par la fenêtre
Une venue de blanc
Dans le bleu de l'air
L'ange qui se pose
Entre ciel et terre
Sur les branchages de l'âme
Un souffle qui demeure
Où je rentre la blancheur
De mes noces ultimes

The airiness of simple, natural presences; the plurality of life, the endless forms of non-selfness yet rising up to meet our ever-ready gaze; being's mysterious colouredness; a coming of presence, presented-ness, that is so delicate, near-mystical, that it is felt as "angelic", a link between soul and physicality, visible and invisible; the image of "breath", reminiscent of Du Bouchet, as is the thematics of whiteness, blueness, air, an image multiple in its connotations and which, here, hints at a circular movement from original breath or spirit and back to such ultimate belonging--such, in brief, are the fascinations of this short *dizain* dominated by 5- and 6-syllable metre, with variations in either direction.

48

A later poem, "Nous créons les traces" (AD, 45), from the section titled "Une illusion d'entrée", merits our attention for several reasons. Firstly, the idea of self-creation fits well into Dohollau's overall poetics, even though, as we have seen, the latter adheres from a different angle to a logic of reception and embrace rather than of forcing and seizure. Secondly, this dovetails with her ethics of love, and again even if such love is *de profil*, not perceived perhaps in all its dimensions. Thirdly, full recognition is given to the grief of existence, although again, and fourthly, compensations are available: cross-cuts, "other" paths, may be short-lived yet revealing of other ontic registers, other "musics", light, lilting, supple... Finally, the question of the divine is posed though without answer. The implication, to my mind, in a poem directly or indirectly evocative of art, and especially the idea of the world as artwork, is deliberately ambiguous: artists, that is, humans, "draw" the exquisiteness of the world divinely; at the same time, there is what can only be called a divineness about the all-absorbing ideal blueness of the sky, both mortal and immortal as a locus of "présences bues". No dogma, but swirling metaphors to convey the equally divine beauties of creation and Creation. The poem "J'écris pour voir..." (AD, 48) comes near to the close of "Une illusion d'entrée". There is not space to do it justice here but I should stress the metaphor of the window of writing; the poetic act of gathering; the reciprocal magnetism of world and word; the so easily mispercieved or bypassed "eternalness" of the ever-present, the depth of our surface being:

> J'écris pour voir ce qui reste à l'extérieur, qui vient s'appuyer contre la vitre du texte. Le presque oublié, attiré par un mot, une couleur, l'air. D'un lieu d'où je me suis retournée pour regarder ailleurs. L'arrière-plan éternel, éternellement au devant de moi.

49

If, then, as this poem and others from *L'Adret du jour* suggest, "[dans] la vie ici / ... voir c'est entrevoir" (AD, 23) and such grills are mental, psychological, emotional and thus screen out much of value, despite our efforts--if this is true, it is equally true that poets and artists seek above all to "ferry over" the things of the world "du visible vers l'invisible / D'une terre sans faille" (AD, 28). No wonder light is such a precious agent for the painter, and such a powerful metaphor for the poet, for its effect and function are not merely banal, utilitarian, but "comme une présence d'ange" (Ad, 40). *Les Portes d'en bas* (1992) pushes still further this intricate interplay between the logics of light and shadow, questions of presence, seeing and love. Light and presence are equated in one of the texts of "Un peintre" (PDB, 13) dedicated to Morandi, but presence still needs the subtleties of shadow to be fully sensed. This, no doubt, is because, for Dohollau as for Hugo, darkness is always inhabited--visually, psychologically, spiritually, etc: it is a *metaphor* of what we are--by light (PDB, 46); and even when whiteness (: that of women's veils) is associated with pain and death, it may be "la lumière d'une absence qui est chemin" (PDM, 50). The aporias of physical seeing, in our bid for some "mastery of the simple" (PDM, 15), thus always seek the balance available through the meta-physical, the inner discovery Dohollau describes of "unsuspected lands" (PDB, 11), dreaming's "taking up of the task" of eyes "qui... / ont vu si peu et mal" (PDB, 10). The full salvatory impact of the seen, the present--"Et le paradis de nouveau se nomme autour des arbres / Dont les feuilles simples rédiment les langues de la terre" (PDB, 43)--depends upon a unified field of perception of our spatio-temporal being-here and *l'invisible*, and this in turn depends upon an "inner sun" of being (PDB, 57), the intuition of some buoyant global logic of being, possibilising and bearing it up, "la flèche qui part et vibre hors de toute cible" Dohollau calls it in "L'Acacia de Constantinople" (PDM, 56-7). Such a logic, or force, or possibilising *gestalt* she seems at times to deem synonymous with love, "le lieu réel" (PDB, 22) and "[le] geste qui sauve en liant tout au tout" (PDB, 66). If Heather Dohollau can say that, "au coin de la rue / Il y a un paradis", this is neither frustrated procrastination nor wishful thinking: such a perception-now of our exquisiteness-now comes from a simple "immersion in the improbable of the heart" (PDB, 66), a recognition that all is already abundantly present, if we but gently open ourselves to it, "sentir... / ... le berceau vide pour une autre naissance" (PDB, 68). The very last poem of *Les Portes d'en bas*, "Soies anciennes" (PDB, 73-4), terminates on a note of quiet, honest self-query, but its entire fabric is woven with the emotions of celebration and adoration despite discreet (metaphors of) recognition of life's difficulties and the looming figure of death itself. Resolutely, but with rare serenity, Dohollau remains

> Attachée par le mince ruban des mots
> Aux mâts des arbres longeant les voix extrêmes
>
> (PDM, 74).

DENISE LE DANTEC

The work of Denise Le Dantec both manifests a considerable range of mode and fascination and maintains a continuity and consistency centred perhaps most significantly around a contemplative, philosophical vision, her passion for the sea and the simple things of the earth, such as its plants and flowers, and, crucially, a strong lyrical strain, seeking exaltation, ecstasy and love where they are neither blatantly available nor in any way absent. Philosopher, painter and poet, Le Dantec gives herself to the multitudinous focal points of lived experience and, although her work from 1980 onwards becomes increasingly poetic in a generic sense, with the publication of *Le Bar aux oiseaux* (1980), *La Vie déserte et quelques lieux* (1980), *Mémoire des dunes* (1985), *Les Fileuses d'étoupe* (1985) and, most recently, *Opuscule d'Ouessant* (1992), I should argue that all her work, including the celebrated *Le Jour* (1975), *Les Joueurs de Go* (1977), and up to *Le Journal des roses* (1991) and *Suite pour une enfance* (1992), retains both an attitude of mind and, frequently, a mode of expression that are intrinsically poetic either in their subject-matter-- madness and its "contents", the marginalised centrality of feminine consciousness, etc.--or in their liberated, tongue-in-cheek yet urgent ironies, or, again, the sheer lyrical desire and availability that can persistently inform them.

Métropole (1970) is Le Dantec's first major collection and is in fact a long single free-verse poem, narrative and discursive in character, though with flagrant ellipses that yet in no way detract from the imaginative, indeed even epic, coherence. We are arguably somewhere near the dreamed intersection of certain poems of Rimbaud's *Saison en enfer*, Eliot's *Wasteland* and Perse's *Anabase*, although there is a more

52

perceptible sparseness attaching to *Métropole*, arising perhaps from the interweaving of a bare (though allegorical) notational style and a crisp, rather philosophically inclined reflectiveness. Despite these latter factors of objectification, the poem remains manifestly emotive, intensely lived, focussed upon telluric and cosmic meaning as mediated by subjective experience. *Métropole* speaks, fundamentally, of the journey towards and the possible construction and occupation of the ultimate city of Beauty. Its point of departure is a consciousness of formlessless (M, 12), solitude, the effacement of language's "radiancy" (M, 13), "un vieux fond de douleur" (M, 33). The quest itself traverses those ever-present nineteenth-century deserts of *le mal*, futility, fear, residual "question", the "monstrousness" of existential "ambiguity" (M, 92). Arrogance and ignorance (M, 24) lie ready to ambush, for the journey remains interior; our "reaching" is a reaching of the self and, psychologically, emotionally, of the other (cf. M, 42). But if nightmare abounds, so does the freedom of (self-)choice and perseverance. Le Dantec's "conclusion" centres upon difficult but feasible self-definition and self-imagination. "Inlassables / nous allions poursuivre / chacun / notre propre figure" (M, 162). The traversal of (one's) being may be plunged into mystery, but it is self-sufficient, adequately salvatory. Early on, even, *Métropole* senses this:

> j'étais
> cette
> adoration
> qui prend du temps
>
> et qui se contredit   (M, 56).

The two books that follow *Métropole--Le Jour* and *Les Joueurs de Go*--remain difficult to classify generically, though they are usually held to be *récits*, despite their avowedly poetic inclinations and, indeed, components. The first of these two volumes focusses attention upon the

53

alienation and madness of women in patriarchal society, the aperception of world and other(ness) that results, the whole poetics of what Le Dantec calls *clôture*. The "Notes pour un scénario imaginaire" that follow and complete the text proper of "Le Jour" constitute not just an "ethical reflection on feminine life" and "un appel à la transgression, au franchissement et à la fulgurance politiques", but, read with what precedes--though the "Notes..." are particularly powerful--an astonishing poetic document of great richness and unsung emotion. A small fragment from "Le Coucher du soleil" (LJ, 57-61) will have to suffice to conjure up these qualities:

> Bientôt reviendra la nuit. Les messages imperceptibles d'étoile à étoile.
> L'univers est plus grand--ou plutôt tout devient parfois si petit. La maison. Le champ. Les toits avoisinants. Et même le soleil.
> La terre est une feuille tremblante et seul ce qui peut être aimé crée la grande ouverture.
> Je vais. Je viens.
> Sur le pas de cette porte. Au bord de l'univers.
>
> (LJ, 59)

Poetry lacks all strict definability, but its presence, here, as throughout *Le Jour*, is unmistakeable: multifacetted, elliptical, leaping with simple meditative or metaphoric impulsiveness from fragment/phenomenon to fragment/phenomenon, trusting blindly to a meaningfulness to come in the midst of greater or lesser delirium or dream or mere observation. The passage from "Notes..." beginning "quand alicia rit.." down to "ni l'écume des mousses--romans" and designated *Un autre poème* (LJ, 156-7), is equally multi-dimensional and mosaical, and thoroughly characteristic of the ramblingly coherent poeticity of this teeming section of the book: we pass, via ellipsis, parataxis, hyperbaton and other figures of disruption and yet forced synthesis, from a friend's laughter at political

54

meetings, through "[le] tremble[ment de] l'été jaune dans ses pierres / qui dans ma bouche oiseau", through "le chat rose albinos et phtisique", through "un vélo renversé dans un talus de violettes", to equally unsituated flashes of consciousness: "et que noir noir le Sénégalais dit / qu'il viendrait quand il pourrait", and, finally, some evocation of collapse and destruction or simple change: "sur la place défoncée / rien ne reste // ni l'acacia // ni l'écume des mousses--romans", ordinary, gentle things erased from existence like so many romanced dreams of beauty.

Les Joueurs de Go, described by Michel Leiris as a kind of "Finnegan's Wake" of French literature, is predicated upon a wild, spontaneous abandonment to "un Imaginaire de Grande instance" (JG, 9). If there is a risk of daftness involved, it is, Le Dantec feels, a risk at once "trivial" and characteristic of all free literary action. Again, as with *Le Jour*, the fundamental power and impulse here are poetic, and textual modes follow. An aesthetics of play and delirium, love and self-liberation dominates, but laughter can turn to irony, even horror, as the contradictions of 1968 become manifest and a poetics of antiviolence leads to darting reflections of good and evil, questions of where to *go*, and why. Without insisting, and before turning to texts perhaps more clearly pertinent to the task at hand, let me quote one of the typical opening sequences of *Les Joueurs de Go*, composed of "lettres brèves fragments notations humeurs états corporels fictions" (JG, 28) and much else:

> aussi lointain qu'aujourd'hui devient hier
> lointaine est la bataille
>
> les oiseaux volent ici et là
> et rien dans leurs cris n'appelle
> ni le passé ni demain

dispersés au souffle du vent, roses, azalées,
les jours et les nuits teintent le ciel de toutes
couleurs

aussi librement
que se déplacent les esprits des joueurs
interminablement
jouant avec les pierres sur le

Go--ban
(JG, 11).

If this sequence does not carry the asocial, but exalted fervour of many other pages, it does show the more reflective and gentle lyrical quality that frames and motivates the splinterings and explosions of *Les Joueurs de Go* and emphasises that this book is no wild generic parenthesis, but rather integrally related imaginatively and modally to, say, *Mémoires des dunes* or *Les Fileuses d'étoupe* to come shortly.

1980 sees the publication of two pieces of work. The first, *Le Bar aux oiseaux*, a libretto, I cannot adequately deal with here, but wish to stress *en passant* its inter- or trans-generic character, for Le Dantec has never sought to concentrate her creative energies within a given realm of performance, nor to stabilise, within a single creation, the generic orientations it may develop. This is true, as we have somewhat seen, for *Le Jour* and *Les Joueurs de Go*, and will continue to be so for various endeavours, including the as yet unpublished *Le Monomotapa ou paroles qui sont déjà du passé*, with its theatrical, musical and narrative-cum-autobiographical modes. *La Vie déserte et autres lieux* is the title given to the diptych that, in 1987, will appear with the twinned titles of "Champ-Bretagne I" and "Champ-Bretagne II". Composed in 1980 and further developed in 1984, these linked poems, orchestrated respectively in nine and twenty suites, in turn often further splay out into smaller sub-units-- this is always true for part I, but often not for part II, where concise,

56

aphoristic structures dominate. "Champ-Bretagne I" is preceded by an epigraph from Empedocles whose light is cast over the entire poem: "Sous le sol, beaucoup de feux sont allumés" (B,40). The specific phenomena of the Breton landscape observed--tilled land, ditches, slopes, sea, crows, roads, mist, stream, trees, wind, etc.--thus bathe in a meditation that transcends whilst earnestly living their somewhat stark immediacy. Le Dantec's sense of being, in, with and between things, at once in separation and a certain continuity, is thus mediated not merely sensually or emotionally. Like poets such as Deguy or Réda, Bonnefoy or Jaccottet, "circumstances" are traversed in many other modes, philosophically, metaphysically, linguistically and so on--though always with grace, lightness of touch, deft evocativeness. Thus do material opaqueness and mental illumination interweave their equal pertinence. Thus do being and the differential analogies (as Ponge would say) of language--its tireless *comme* and *comme si*, the many *peut-être* of its mere semblances (cf. B, 40-44)--meld their "hereness" and their profoundly alterity, their finiteness and their infinite expansiveness. To caress the "givenness" of the world is to traverse its mystery symbolically. The self-writing of things-as-things still urges upon us a reading of signs whose meanings, finally, remain to be taken up, infinitely, within each shifting self. The ploughed clods of earth thus become:

Mottes-visions. Mottes-songeries.

Reliquat du *"cher corps"* de la "si pauvre âme".

(B, 44)

As the close of part I suggests, for "the unique, extreme, scattered obliqueness of the Field" to be intuited (B, 44), it must be traversed, travelled, despite the rocky, crumbling path that narrowly winds through it in the rain.

None of this should lead us to believe that Denise Le Dantec's work, in *La Vie déserte* or elsewhere, is charged with a complex symbolism needing patient unravelling. The opposite is true, if anything. But, as the opening of part II indicates, "le questionnement surgit de partout... non paix, non possession. Difficile de faire face, le soir, quand il n'y a plus que le ciel" (B, 45). A deep reflectiveness ensues, steeped in bodily experience and psychological projection, and caught up in the slippage of all being that provokes, even constitutes, permanent query: "On va d'un moment naturel à un autre moment naturel. //...// Cela interroge de façon drastique. C'est l'interrogation même" (B, 45). The brushing of the self up against the teeming, changing phenomena of being, thus may lead to the experience of their "glory" and "sublimity", but it can also be lived as a more violent "confrontation" (cf. B, 45). Uncertainty, danger, exile may mushroom forth, the "ordinary" may become a locus of "risk", a "disappearance of meaning" quickly resulting (cf. B, 45-6). To turn towards the outside, otherness, is, in effect, to realise an "absence" underpinning all "presence", and to understand the inseparability of self and other, observer and observed. "C'est cela que l'on ressent: on n'est pas séparé du plus intime de soi" (B, 46). "Champ-Bretagne II" concludes with an elliptical meditation of beauty and its implicit relation to this discourse of observer/observed, self/other. The inconspicuousness, the utter simplicity, of beauty is held to be extremely pertinent to Le Dantec's conception and practice of poetry and writing in general. Such "simplicity" is not merely structural, intellectual, aesthetic, however, it is equally ethical. Linked to her poetics of questioning, it seems synonymous with an unpretentiousness that yet remains enquiring. "L'humilité est ce mouvement [de l'être / de l'art] qui nous conduit au niveau de notre condition mortelle" (B, 48).

Just as 1980 witnesses a flurry of poetic energy, so, in 1985, does Denise Le Dantec achieve a further provisional summit with the publication of what may be regarded as two of her finest poetic collections, both appearing with Folle Avoine: *Mémoire des dunes* and *Les Fileuses d'étoupe*. The opening pages of the first of these two elegant metaphorical meditations reveal a visually alert poet, attuned to the subtleties of land- and marine-scape, yet understanding that all is in large measure inner, psychological space, "un champ de mémoire, / intact, / qui se retire" (MD, 1). Bare, stark beauties emerge, "stries / sur le gris arraché / à l'extrême du pays" (MD, 1) or "ramures / sur l'étendue du sable" (MD, 3), always economically captured, known to be caught up in the swirl of time and memory as well as the sensuousness of language in its mysterious relation to being and origin:

> le mot humecté de salive
>
> de tout ce qui commence   (MD, 3).

Mémoire des dunes proceeds to develop an open poetics of distance and reminiscence, absence and presence, often dwelling upon the doubled sense of separation words can produce despite the poet's contemplative recourse to them: "la phrase écrit sa phrase / dans la phrase" (MD, 5). Despite the simplicity, the (ironic or honest) naiveness, of the writer's or the painter's "gesture" (MD, 6), space's "intimacy" suggests a consciousness of the delicacy of all secondary seizure of being. But, although strong emotions such as fear (MD, 6) can be drawn into the equation and a "poverty" can be experienced due to the "absent alphabets" blocking decipherment (MD, 9), Le Dantec knows that a "seeing" is feasible within the inner opaqueness:

Au noir de l'oeil,
dans l'épars,
plantation de racines
le sable s'ouvre
pour voir   (MD, 8).

Some poems record directly the real, without any veiling feeling of linguistic or emotional limitation: "Immense..." (MD, 11), "De tertre en tertre" (MD, 12) or the exquisitely simple "Étoile de mer":

Étoile de mer,
posée,

en extase

sur le chemin   (MD, 13).

Perhaps it is those (experiences of) things that can "cause [words] to shine" (MD, 10) that allow for such transparency, such immediate transitiveness; perhaps such privileged, uncluttered experiences of things are part of "la grande parole liquide" (MD, 15) that already inhabits and articulates being--and that, presumably, poetic expression merely fleetingly, intuitively, taps into. Certainly Denise Le Dantec is wonderfully sensitive to the magnificent natural fusion of the elements of our being--birds, light, the sea air, for example--and sees therein some "signature", some sign-ification that "l'oiseau signe / avec la lumière // et l'aile encore humide // [qui] vole dans l'air marin" (MD, 16). Such meaning--traces, movements, semiosis--defies all specificity whilst being rooted in specificity: it is part of what Le Dantec calls that visible and yet inconspicuous "contrée / du rien et du multiple" (MD, 17). The banal thus bathes forever in the magicalness, the improbable *féerie* of a cosmic immensity to which the poet has always been and will always be--as *Suite pour une enfance* will show--exceptionally alert:

```
        Sous l'entrepôt d'étoiles
        les caissons

        versent

        dans la magie          (MD, 19).
```

Thus, also, does the ephemeral wed the eternal, "[l'écume] à peine fleurie" (MD, 21) its very possibility; thus does "ce segment d'océan tombé en déshérence" (MD, 25), as the final poem of *Mémoire des dunes* expresses it, achieve--via the "blue obscureness" of conversation, of poetic expression--a relation with "the immense" that "neither stupour nor hope" adequately explain (MD, 24).

Les Fileuses d'étoupe is undoubtedly Denise Le Dantec's most accomplished poetic production to date and is honoured, in 1985, with the Prix de poésie de la Société des Gens de Lettres. As with those of *Mémoire des dunes*, these poems are lyrical poems, exalted but discreet, personal yet linked to the world's vastness, its mystery and its mythicalness. The liminal text, "Ah ce voyage en Cornouailles..." (FE ,2), exposes in a largely more full-bodied unrhymed free-verse form than that espoused in *Mémoire des dunes*, a poetics that will develop further, of both observation and desire, recording of the lived and scriptural insufficiency, acceptance and unacceptability. The task is at once anecdotal and manifestly desirous of that Reverdyan anti-anecdotality or *antinature*--or "intrinsic" poeticalness--that, *grosso modo*, all modern French poetry will seek to establish. The second text, "Maigres, assises,..." (FE, 3), plunges unequivocally into this second, modern mode which, undoubtedly, gives to the collection its driving and lasting power:

```
        Maigres, assises, jambes ouvertes sur les talus,
        Les fileuses d'étoupe lapent leurs assiettées de givre
        Leurs yeux creux ne voient ni blé ni vache
        dans ce terrain pierreux et froid
```

Entre l'os et la peau, il n'y a rien
Rien entre le lit de pierres et l'eau

D'autres à Camlann ou à Portsmouth

Naviguant pour toujours dans les mers allongent leurs doigts

Que ne suis-je Oiseau d'Owein
Pour du haut du ciel excrémenter la neige?

--Deviens telle que je te trouverai quelque part

We are straightaway in the domain of an atemporality that has gathered to it all the concreteness of the temporal: feminine presences, spinning and creating from coarse, minimal substance; there--suddenly there--in their bony sensualness, their stark vulnerability; outside and inside resemble each other in their cold, bare reduction, yet such minimality is matched by a sense of the eternalness, the ever-journeying of these mythical *fileuses d'étoupe*. The poem ends with the poet's desire to plunge still further into myth, a real beyond the real, to seek a freedom of motion at once physical and symbolic (:scriptural: the wild *joueuse de go*'s flagrant blackening of the white). And yet, in fulfilling this desire a need remains for (self-)recognition in this re-formed/deformed space beyond space.

Many other imaginative factors develop and freely interact in the fifty or so poems of *Les Fileuses d'étoupe*. Le Dantec reveals a keen sensitivity to the tensions, the "spasms" (FE, 4), the sharp, often paradoxical movements of being in time and space, and the tale of love the book both flickeringly and intensely recounts is naturally situated in the midst of telluric and cosmic immensity: "Nue sur une terre d'aiguilles / et sous les vents / Entraînant les nuages et les loups" (FE, 7). The linked, rhythmic principles of weaving and unravelling, forming and unforming, that are felt to animate the earth, are thus not surprisingly understood to characterise emotional, psychological event: little wonder that the magic of the poet's encounter with *l'Ange*, already caught up in a violent swiftness, can move back and forth between metaphors of *L'Ange noir* and *Saint-Ange*, wretchedness and healing, enmity and ecstasy, "hellishness" and "magnitude" (FE, 29). The experiences--for although one, they are multiple--narrated thus ally themselves to the great sensory-sensual-sexual symbols describing all earthly life: metaphors of flowering and sun-ripened fructification (FE, 8,15,16,26); acts of embrace, of gift and receipt; signs of farewell; invocation of "[le] visible et [l']invisible / Dans la douceur d'ordures de notre terre" (FE, 31);invocation, too, great, magnificent appeal to the great half-real, half-mythical "black birds of Gwendollen", the "crows of Owein", and so on, in the splendid "O oiseaux de Rhiannon" (FE, 38-9), seeking the reinvigoration of the self, poetically, materially, pshychologically. The collection terminates moreover with an expression of generosity towards the other and a sense of the earth's constant "incarnation" (FE, 52). The final poem (FE, 54) merits an attention it can barely be given here:

> Passent les grands charrois d'automne, l'amour, la neige,
>   le viol et les grands froids
> Tous les forfaits du coeur, toutes les mélancolies,
> L'Ardeur inoubliable de tout ce qui fut beau,
>   égaré comme les feuilles sur les glèbes,
> Passent les sens et les soupirs de l'Ange
> Sur les chemins immenses, de l'autre côté du monde,
> Et l'angoisse de nos rêves marqués de cet amour
>
> Des quatre points du monde jaunis sous la
>   tourmente
> Les yeux ne servent plus
>
> A peine si on décèle la Vierge dans le Loup

A poetics of passage or passingness clearly dominates in this closing text of an avowedly Taoistically inclined poet, where all is seen as swept along by the poignancy of time, silently and splendidly, in equivalence and perhaps implicitly according to some unnameable equity. Thus is it that the exquisite touchingness of the beautiful is scattered, along with all our sadnesses, over the glebe, in a vast, moving flow of all of life--its personal *summa*, its infinite, imperceptible meanings. Difficulty is part of this flow, but its anguish and torment are carried off by it, though imposing conditions of bare continuity and stuttering vision of innocence in the midst of ruse and preying. Le Dantec's closing words bring both sobriety, then, and yet an impressive sereneness. It is not resignation that is produced here, I should argue, but a sense of life as a vast mosaical becoming, at once uplifting and dismaying. Let us not forget, however, that this poem is buoyed up by Denise Le Dantec's poetics of "spinning" and by the counter-myth of the magical power of the "birds of Rhiannon". "The eyes [may] no longer serve", but no poet is without infinite resource.

After *Les Fileuses d'étoupe* come, in particular, *Le Roman des jardins de France* (1987), written with Le Dantec's architect brother, Jean-Pierre, and demonstrating the poet's delight in imbricating modes of documentation and imagination, material factuality and lyricism, observation and projection, verifiable alterity and lived subjectivity; and *Le Journal des roses* (1991), with its not dissimilar fusing of historical and personal insights, its provision in diary form, less of a structured chronology than a multifocussed and constantly decentred story of the rose, of roses, in all their affectively intricate, half-real, half-mythical, allegorical presence and pertinence. If expert horticulturalists are evoked, so too are poets, philosophers, novelists, princesses, kings, musicians, artists. The story of a massive collective fascination, in becoming a journal, hesitates between fragmentation and continuity, the depth of a life-time obsession and affinity, and the intensity and relative impetuousness of a released day-by-day creation over two years (1987-88). Denise Le Dantec thus succeeds in seizing something of the "other" of the rose, its unspokenness, its deeper cultural and natural mystery, in her spontaneously vast and cumulative, though equally meditated and researched mosaic. The book--which is a kind of open, latticed artwork of the rose--generates, finally, but non-reductively, a delicate and multiple world poetics of the rose, though a poetics never objectified, platitudinously exteriorised, remaining as it does enmeshed with a personal vision that never effaces itself to the advantage of some pure conceptual but illusory construct. A poem, in a way Deguy might conceive it, beyond generic delimitation.

1992 sees the publication of a slim, but significant poetical *plaquette*, *Opuscule d'Ouessant*, to which in closing I should like to offer warm praise and some modicum of evaluation. The volume's smallness, its unpretentiousness, is not, firstly, without significance; nor is the stress placed upon special place and that point where the intangible meets the tangible in our lived experience. Denise Le Dantec opts for prose poems here, short texts with either two or three paragraphs, most containing one simply punctuated sentence or *verset* only. Gone are the unrhymed and almost completely unpunctuated free-verse forms of distinctly varying length that grace the pages of *Les Fileuses d'étoupe*; gone, too, the truly compact, elliptical though linked verses of *Mémoire des dunes*, where, oddly however, a prefiguration of the prose mode of *Opuscule* can be had in the closing two poems, "Nous conversons..." and "Et de ce pays fatal" (MD, 24-5). Imaginatively speaking, nevertheless, there is a great deal of continuity between the three collections, and, indeed, other work, not only the *La Vie déserte et autres lieux* but the contemporaneous *Suite pour une enfance* (1992): wind, sea, rain, birds, sunlight, dawn, the ordinary, for

65

many half-forgotten elements and movements of being, and, of course, the inevitable reflections, sparse yet haunting, that accompany all. Here is the opening poem (00,1):

> Seuls, le vent--cet excès--et la pluie sur ma face... Le jour se lève dans le reflux.
>
> Dernière moi, les oiseaux de mer tombent et crient.
>
> --Où sont ceux-là qui s'abreuvaient ici?

In the poems that follow, characteristic attention is given to the earth's transmutations, the breaking up and dispersal of stones, for example; to the mists and gloom that Le Dantec equally relates to temporal factors; to, also, the metaphoric, psychological value of the concrete, of a sea-storm, for example: "Pour un peu, ce serait le cri du monde" (OO, 3). "Autour de soi, c'est sombre, instable, inquiet", as Le Dantec writes in the fifth poem (OO, 5), which thus quickly establishes itself as a physically descriptive utterance, whose designation yet far outstrips the landscapes before her. The constant seething of waters is somehow impressive emotionally, spiritually, but the ellipses and rushes of the poem allow for a deft skipping beyond such possibly clinging implications to, for example here, the idea of the now-ness of all phenomenality, all being: "une vague a absorbé toutes les vagues" (OO, 5), reflects Le Dantec in true Taoist abolition or condensation of the disquietude initially evoked. The poem "Oh chante l'armoise dans les décombres!" (OO, 6) similarly matches abandonment with brilliance, the latter absorbing the former in still tense but oddly tranquil assent: "ce buisson étrange qui redonne son éclat à tout ce qu'on délaisse: soleil d'os, de brindilles et d'arêtes de poisson" (OO, 6). Moving through and with the things of the earth thus entails a reflection that restores caress and gentleness where neglect has so often reigned. "Comment ne songerais-tu pas", she asks herself, "à ce point de braise qui tombe en cendre à chacun de tes pas?" (OO, 7): if the links to Jaccottet or Dohollau seem strong, wider, perhaps endless, poetic, affinities also come to mind: Ponge, Guillevic, Bancquart, Perse. If, however, it is partly through such caress and thought that things may be "raised to the level of prayer" (OO, 8), Le Dantec still remains deeply disturbed at times by the jostling, bustling effect of being: "Tu as beau t'écrier: ce qui vient heurte en toi ce qui hésite et tremble" (OO, 8). The "glory" of existence, of sea, heathland, grasses is a fine compensation, but it cannot quite rid her of the "brutality" of the buffeting wind (OO, 10); nor of an inherent ontological discomfort at not really knowing "how to live in this mortal knowledge" (OO, 9). A sense of Taoist flow and mingling of being's comings and goings, doings and undoings, reaffirms itself in the haunting last poem, "Et tout se mêle..." (OO, 12), yet opaqueness dominates consciousness and psychology is only fragilely serene at best. The lovely *Suite pour une enfance*, an autobiographical *récit* of great delicacy and perception, equally strikes this note of precarious though mature equilibrium and consenting abandonment, but the grief its pages may contain--this Denise Le Dantec both knows and wills--attains to a "shining" transcendence writing still paradoxically can achieve (SPUE, 154).

JANINE MITAUD

The poetic *oeuvre* of Janine Mitaud, that Char was to recognise in 1965 with his foreword to *L'Echange des colères*, stretches back over fifty years to the vigorous and moving war poems of *Hâte de vivre*, appearing in 1949. The title would seem clearly to project urgent ontic desire and socio-spiritual need. The liminal poem, "Pour une prière" (HV, 9), is, as its own title suggests, less a full-blown prayer than a kind of prolegomenon or preliminary, temporarily unamplifiable gesture, which, whilst sensitive to place, earth, germination and growth, finds itself entrenched, though in August, in wintry devastation (it is August 1942). Incarnation dovetails with crucifixion; eternity perhaps has slipped to synonymity with void; we hover, as the poem concludes, between oblivion, a need for new "worthiness" and a dream--but no reality-- of some christic peace, appeasement and redemption.

The remaining twenty poems of *Hâte de vivre*, varying in length from twelve to forty occasionally rhymed and metrically largely free-verse lines, progress chronologically--each text is dated--up to mid-May, 1949. If this permits a kind of "historical" reading of the collection, it should be stressed that, despite a movement towards hope and increased feasibility, all poems remain tensional and alert to the fragility of existential and poetic accomplishment. This said, it is also true that Mitaud is conscious from the outset of the arguable simplicity of all resolution: a listening to the love within the self that may lead to a "secret yielding up of the world" (cf. HV, 12). What largely dominates throughout is the blatant contradiction between the "divine" pulsing rhythms of the universe and the violence of lives (HV, 13), between the terrible memory of wretchedness (HV, 15) and the yet dancing, rebounding energy of "le présent [qui] brûle" (HV, 19), swept constantly as it is by the "wind of the infinite" (HV, 20). Determination and trust slowly grow by the month and the year: "Le soleil des charniers doit mûrir des bourgeons" (HV, 26) is an astonishing and moving expression of a willed fate intensely lived in the intimacy of metaphor Mitaud, like Jaccottet, would have viscerally, *really*, lived and shared. The closing poems, too, exude a sense, in the midst of a generalised destruction of the "religious", of some emergent centre or *noyau*: a religion of self-(re)creation, corporeal and spiritual, beyond narcissism, beyond linguistic and aesthetic nicety: "*Ecoute mon cri*", she writes in "J'étais simple..." (HV, 32-3), "*Je me reconstruis / ... / Ah que j'ai pouvoir de t'aimer / Pour trouver le temps de bâtir*". "La Boussole" (HV, 34) rounds out the collection and is, clearly, a poem of possible orientations upon and with the earth, a poem of new telluric adventure, intimate, collective--"et nos pas entament la terre" is the open-ended closure articulated--not self-protective, retreating into some form of idealising, illusory perfection and "infallibleness". "Blessure et pain / Lutte et lumière", with love as magnetic North and language forming "par constellations drues / Autour de l'intégrité du noyau". Life and poetry in ceaseless motion, forever "se met[tant] en branle".

Départs (1952) is the next major collection of Janine Mitaud, appearing as it does, like *Hâte de vivre*, with Seghers, after the publication in 1951 of some more slender small-press collections such as *Bras étendus* and *Silence fabuleux*. The title would seem to echo the purpose generated at the close of *Hâte de vivre*, but only in the broadest sense of movement and availability might we wish to connect the poetics of *Départs* to those of, say, a Baudelaire or a Mallarmé, or even a Rimbaud. The collection's opening untitled poem I quote both better to convey the latter divergence and to show that, despite the gains of *Hâte*

69

de vivre, tensions are not glibly dissipated, a continued consciousness remaining of personal and collective challenge:

> Gonflés de manne dérisoire
> Les poings des vagues crèvent
> Contre les plages en plongée
>
> Repos léger des corps
> Salubres vacances
> A la rumeur des continents
> Que le sang dérange
> Et dans la séculaire odeur
> Des sacrifices et des charniers modernes
>
> Grâce à la déraison du monde
> Le soleil comme un trou au-dessous de ton coeur.

(D, 9)

Images of uneasiness, anxiety and intense contradiction jostle with a sense of increased ease. The modernity evoked is, of course, staggeringly distinct from that of, say, Apollinaire's earlier poetry, just as the *déraison* conjured is far from the experimental poetic projects of the youthful Rimbaud. No evasion, here, of the terrible, still much-lived aftermath of the Second World War, and the "charnel-house sun" of *Hâte de vivre*, rather than sparking improbable resurrection, now represents an affective destruction that helps explain the "derisoriness" of the heavenly manna the poem liminally conveys. The very idea, then, of departure appears to be plunged into irony, if we assume it to imply positively connoted discovery and renewal. The poems that follow may thus erase all dates of composition, but the character of psychological reality persists. And yet, lucidly, guardedly, patiently, in varyingly long structures of free blank verse (with the exception of "Chanson pour Monique", D, 18), Janine Mitaud edges her way back towards those forces she knows to be necessary for mere continuation, let alone transmutation: hope, faith in youth, in that "strange, dense language" welling up within her, with its

70

"flashing risks" and yet its implicit "will for happiness" (cf. D, 12) that a Bonnefoy will later powerfully preconise. Slowly, then, a poetics of departure does emerge into clarity, for we understand it to depend not just upon desire and will, but upon the very vulnerability or open recognition the opening poem articulated. "Peut-on s'abriter aux musiques de frairie..." is the incipit of a poem without title (D, 14); the question it poses is implicitly answered in the negative: (self-)sheltering is not the course Mitaud perceives as valid, tempting though it may briefly be. The collectivity's feasible fraternal transmutations are made clear in the poem's conclusion:

> Mais votre voix majeure demeurée
> Prend l'envergure des oiseaux
> Chasse l'automne et l'habitude
> Par libres orages de fraîcheur et de foudre

Going forth into the stormy but reinvigorating liberation of the self by the self, here is a project worthy of us all. Its articulation, moreover, seems to release much fresh energy: the social allegory of "Le Pays des merveilles" (D, 15); songs for, and of, named women, wherein a full consciousness is reaffirmed that "mon amour me crée / Au centre calme de la roue" (D, 9); a post-Claudel, pre-Bellow "naming of the day", an establishment of (poetic) action in the ever-possible *hic et nunc* (D, 20). "Le Poème" (D, 23) may begin by evoking difficulty and the paradoxes of destruction, violence and menace, but "progress", "presence" and a "silence" from which new voice may emerge quickly affirm their logics and show that the poem, as it in fact concludes, may attain to "l'éclair d'une cinquième saison". Not dissimilarly, the death of Paul Eluard occasions not grief but a gratitude for the light shed by "le long rayon de ta vie" (D, 24). Images proliferate of spurting and budding, of "le vent charri[ant] une sauvage liberté" (D, 27), and the volume concludes with

71

a Bonnefidian insistence upon the metaphor--and reality--of the child "questing in glory / An invincible sun", discovering within "la marque indélébile de la lumière" (D, 31).

L'Echange des colères (1965), illustrated by Casazza and prefaced by a Char much affected by the "féconds bienfaits" of Mitaud's "profound", "receptive" and "original" writing, might be thought of as a pivotal work, both crowning all that has been accomplished to date and looking ahead to the mature developments to come. Poetry is seen as an act of witness, social and spiritual, as a desire to penetrate the world's profundity, as both confrontation and virtual extolment. "La parole affronte la mort Le verbe crie / Son besoin d'une terre et d'un magnificat" (EC, 5), Mitaud exclaims in the collection's liminal text. Language may be plagued with blindness, yet it thus retains capacity, combating waste and "brokenness", orienting itself towards a future that both recognises cosmic tensions and gives itself to the earth's intrinsic "generosity" and self-confident elaborations (EC, 9). Transmutation, fructification, a reliance upon the "eternal" within the ephemeral--such are the existential mechanisms intuited by Janine Mitaud and that explain the degree to which "comme un vin me tente le verbe": poetic language as the exalted, but felt and lucid conveyor of the earth's endlessly potential "semences d'actes de lumière" (EC, 16). Pain, anguish and "holocausts" can thus be rectified by the language of "mes immenses désirs", by "l'imaginaire [qui] est prêt (EC, 18, 23).

Various poems push vigorously and far this poetics of renewal and rethought being. "Comme une arme" (EC, 24) metaphorises sky and light in their redynamising, resurrectional action, and figures (wo)man as, precisely, the centre of a crucial figuration or "dreaming" of existence. "Monde je suis..." (EC, 26) is the poem of self-world fusion or interconnection, of poetic (=[self-]creative) questing after "le chatoiement de vérité", of seeing, vision and future:

> J'entends l'amour franchir l'apparence des corps
>
> Ainsi naissant de nos premières vies
> Sans doute serons-nous substance merveilleuse
> Plus proches plus conscients de l'amande éblouie

And "La Sphère" (EC, 31) speaks vividly of the moving cycles of terrestrial accomplishment, whilst evoking "le cercle... nouveau que tu as fait franchir / A ton propre univers durci et délivré", and conjuring the firm, culminating vision of a further dreamed accomplishment, "liv[ing] star or fruit amongst fruits", even well beyond the self's mortality.

L'Echange des colères thus seeks to articulate the poet's movement "towards the meaning of the world", now and in all the nows beyond. Shifting networks and fermentations are sensed everywhere, for life is seen as nothing if not surging creativity, rendering presence "fulgurante et familière" (EC, 38). Atrocities and wounds are currently part of this surging, but so, too, are dream, thought and outcry (cf. EC, 47), constant renascence, the intensity of our "absolute Julys" (EC, 67), "l'opulence de l'amour" (EC, 78) and a sense of our multidimensional being despite the difficulties of individuality (cf. EC, 70). "Rythme des étés" (EC, 75) is a splendid poem of trust and vision, a poem that, like "Vivre", affirms the degree to which love is our absolute "river", the true place of our ontic flowingness and our natural meaning.

La Porte de la terre (1969) and *La Parole naturelle* (1971) provide varying clarification as to the nature and feasibility of the vision contained in *L'Echange des colères*. The quite substantial 1969 volume I cannot do justice to here, but would briefly focus attention upon three in many respects emblematic poems: the liminal "La Porte de la terre", "Amour"

73

and "Adolescents l'hiver" (PT, np). The first of these poses the question of telluric access--of entry to the occulted yet sensed meaning of the earth, and, implicitly, of the self, via the very processes of entry. The poem's teeming metaphors, its delight in alliteration and anaphora, make this an at once opaque and rhythmically powerful poem of love of the mortal, the simple yet dazzling "énigme de flamme et d'eau", ancient, timeless, yet ever-manifest. Mitaud's "vision", here, is predicated on a love for things, yet beyond them, so pulsional as to be almost blinding in its symbolic scope and visceral intensity:

> Un amour né pour crépiter de becs d'orage
> Et savourer les grêles d'alises gelées
> Pour délivrer la vigne incendiée d'alcool
>
> Né pour franchir dans l'éboulis des vents
> rompus la dernière cassure

The second poem I shall evoke, "Amour", arguably gathers within it the same strands of a vision clearly sensual, ethical, but equally mystical or, if one prefers, psychically alert in its implications. Ellipsis multiplies here and images still persist of "flames, snakes and salamanders". Poetry, symbolic of all vital action in and upon the world, is intimately bound up with truth--which is both "flèche et but"--and factors of unity, soul-intervention and "consecration" draw Mitaud's imagination powerfully. Her vision here entails a strangely beautiful fusing, spiritual but almost (al)chemical too: "Cernés surpris", she writes, "Nous devenons l'avers et le revers / D'une même monnaie solaire :/ L'intense dessin nous perpétue en feu". An ontology of shifting, mingling energies thus finally dominates; consumption and self-expenditure become synonymous with self-generation and self-perpetuation. The third poem, "Adolescents l'hiver", dedicated to Char, offers complexities and subtleties I can only hint at here: the quivering flora and fauna of childhood developing through the

74

mystery of the psyche's expansion; "[le] tourbillon laiteux [qui dort] dans les bagues de transparence" of being and langauge; the acrobatic juggling of adolescent existence "sur la ligne mélodique / De l'inexprimable"; love's brief, flashing experience of eternity; the "implacable grace" of life's youthful resurrections; the ever-available "riverbed" of being "[qui] fuit / Vers les fruits // Ouvr[e] l'aube comme un vaste vitre". Cascade upon cascade of metaphor, Reverdyan rather than phantasmagorically surrealist, wherein vision remains intensely, prophetically, but openly ethical, spiritual.

La Parole naturelle, on the other hand, taken up again the 1974 *Danger*, suggests that poetic language and the vision at once underpinning and underpinned by it, perform in function of a developed patience and that earlier mentioned blindness which turns out to constitute a prescience. These are arguably the ingredients of imagination, the "imaginary [that] is ready", for together they represent a capacity for dreaming the real, for a divination based in "un alphabet de pulsations légères" (D, 67). Thus is it that Janine Mitaud can, though "démunie / [...,] accueill[ir] l'essentiel" (D, 65) and, "count[ing] upon light proofs", achieve "une évidence de poème" (D, 69). Joy, furthermore, is shown to be linked to possibility, its brilliant "chance" allowing access to deep presence within time's frothiness (cf. D, 61), just as the unsaid may grow into speech within the obscure recesses of consciousness. Char's poetics of compactness is thus espoused--"un vain lyrisme fuit / Devant vérité nue Sérénité brûlante et fraîche" (D, 64)--for its dense and "naturally" metaphorised minimalism, its craggy, bony tenderness, is deemed better able to avoid the traps of high rhetoric or convoluted intellection. The unpretentiousness of silence, coupled with an unflagging sense of being's inherent "évidence heureuse / [...,] m'élève à la parole naturelle" (D, 79).

Danger is eloquently prefaced by Pierre Seghers. "Sans cesse renaissante", he writes of Mitaud, "sans répit criblée, émigrante de la patience à la poursuite de la vraie vie, elle est chant profond, canto-jondo, essentiel éclat du quotidien, honneur et défi, âpre langage maîtrisé". Despite its title and underlying problematics, the book constantly catalyses negation, seeking to "dégrader le temps banal / en faveur d'une éternité" (D, 12), to ever recommence being, to foment the soul's "indiscipline" in the face of all that would "outlaw" it (D, 17). Such refusal and the social critique that *Danger* generates, are of course the signs of Mitaud's willed "recomposition" of being (D, 35); their struggle is but the other face of a more serene and ideal consent. Poetry, ultimately, is transparent, unlimited, maternal, universal, giving, the bearer of cosmic meaning (cf. D, 40)--for, not only does Mitaud argue that, beyond the specificities (albeit unlimiting), "au-delà du vocable / [,] bouillonne la source" (D, 50)--that is, what truly orients her vision--but, further, her very being is multiple, beyond simple notions of incarnation and thus mortality: "Je suis plusieurs je m'arrache à la division / des miroirs" (D, 53). It is more or less at this point of the collection that the texts of *La Parole naturelle* insert themselves into *Danger*'s discourse. The closing section of the volume, "Le Point d'orgue", elects to stress the remarkable "luxury" of life's endless and inconspicuous experiences (cf. D, 88 "c'est l'heure..."), their sensuality, their concreteness, but also the 'warmth of the mystery" with which they wrap us round (D, 85).

1979 sees the publication, after that of *Le Soleil sursoit* (1974) and *Juillet plain-chant* (1977), of one of Janine Mitaud's most powerful and exquisite works, *Livre-poème*. Written as one single, continuous poem, now in prose, now in free verse, exploiting the teeming resources of typographical order and white space, italics and capitalisation, quotation and incompletion, non-contextualisation and rich metaphoricity, the book constitutes a deep personal triumph of emotion and spirit. *"Alors se lève"*, Mitaud writes, *l'apocalypse de la terreur vaincue"* (LP, 23): a triumph of love over fear, meaning over nonsense, future and presence over finality. *Livre-poème* is thus "ce travail absurde en lequel nous avons foi" (LP, 7), the working out of poetic crisis through poetry itself. Its scattered, quasi-Mallarméan signs--but there is more semantic cement and more referential sap--resemble the stars in the dark enigma of the night sky: "Cette volée de cendres éblouissantes, c'est un code. Par ces abîmes, ces semences, sache que le désespoir sert de négatif" (LP, 9). Existential catastrophe, absurdity and despair thus yield to the intoxification of survival, courage and love, assent to that "secret central" that (even) trees so discreetly, so surely, project (cf. LP, 21):

> menaces, dents et dards s'ensevelissent sous une méticuleuse splendeur.   (LP, 21)

Thus is it, too, that Mitaud's poem gathers increasing psychological momentum, "burst[ing] the bubble of dementia" (LP, 32); collapsing time and space into action-now; "se déplo[yant], messianique, / imminent comme l'éclair: / le paraphe des défis / court de l'égarement jusqu'à la lumière" (LP, 33); excorcising "murders" and transcending contradiction and difference (LP, 36); leaping beyond "infirm [image]" (LP, 46) and a representation of the world precariously recognised as based in total "ignorance" (LP< 47-8). *Livre-poème* manages to become the realised mental act of self-renascence--"voici le vert fondamental", Mitaud cries out (LP, 26)--and, as such, achieves presence, whilst being, too, the poem of advent. "Je porte sans repos" she writes near the book's close, "le sac de brume / où couvent, sous le gris, / les révélations"(LP, 46). "Investigation" has thus triumphed over anguish, but assisted by both an

77

"affirm{ation], / dans la sèche fatalité, [du] toujours scandaleux amour"
(LP, 50), and a vision never deserting Mitaud:

> Rien n'est égaré de ce que je ne perçois plus
> Rien ne coule au néant de ce que je ne puis discerner
> encore.   (LP, 49)

Three years later, in 1982, appears the elegant short collection *De
la rose à l'éros*. As its title suggests and as certain poems demonstrate,
there is in Mitaud--*Suite baroque* will shortly confirm and further explore
this--a fascination with the incessantly feasible slippages of language,
morphological, semantic slippages, but slippages speaking of the endless
imbrications of the real, its Baudelairian correspondences and deep unity,
its "secret affinities" so manifest to Gautier. "Les signes glissent de l'un
à l'autre mot", she writes, "d'un cri à l'autre // Le son le sens / de la rose
à l'éros / à l'essor du héros" (RE, 14). Such a fascination, then, as with
Baudelaire and Gautier, far from leading to some poetics of gratuitous
textual autotelism or sheer ludicity, reanchors language's swarmingness
within a non-linguistic depth bearing it up. "Les mots ne riment que par
/ leurs substances profondes / jamais par jeu" (RE, 6). What remains
central is underlying, buoyant meaning, "signification de fleuve / exigence
de terre / soleil ésotérique", as she clarifies in "Si ce nom..." (RE, 29),
all channelling speech, however, to what she terms an "initiation à la
trinité des / valeurs telluriques". Such tellurism is firmly bound up with
a logic of what she calls "la chaleur des âmes inextinguibles" (RE, 17)
and this lived fusion urges her to express the need to rethink our old
ironies, scepticisms and despairs in a movement, again Baudelairian, as
Fusées and *Mon cœur mis à nu* amply show, towards difficult
"divination... / assimilable au plus haut amour" (RE, 30). Grace and
danger characterise poetic utterance, Mitaud insists in her closing text, no

doubt in accordance with the logic of the volume's opening: "Je demeure / du côté des sèves non contrariées / Mais reflétant le meurtre / je brûle / et le brûle" (RE, 5).

Suite baroque (1983), immaculately published, like *Livre-poème*, by Pierre Fanlac, also rises to the exceptional poetic heights of the earlier volume. It differs from *Livre-poème*, however, in that it offers a characteristic collation of separate texts, but it retains the tendency--that will dissipate somewhat with *Poèmes cruels* and notably with *Pages*--to develop broader poetic sweeps, the two shortest poems being of 8 lines, many others being in the mid-length range (2 x 10, 2 x 11, 4 x 12, 2 x 13, 1 x 14, 5 x 15, 2 x 16, 1 x 17, 1 x 18, 1 x 19, 2 x 20), yet others extending increasingly beyond such typical contemporary compactness: 2 x 22 lines, 1 x 25, 1 x 26, 2 x 28, 1 x 31, 2 x 32, 1 x 35, 2 x 40, 1 x 41, 2 x 45. This does not mean, however, that the mid-length or longer poems are consistently composed of unbroken textual blocks or the Lamartinian 20-line stanzas of his *Jocelyn* or *La Chute d'un ange*. Compact and highly varied stanzaic structure is rife and obeys impulsive discipline, personal rhythm, as does the equally fluctuating line-length of *Suite baroque*--a fluctuation rarely reaching, however, to the 15-, 16- or 17-syllable *verset* and thus stabilising itself within the freedom of nevertheless traditional rhythmic voice.

At the imaginative level, Mitaud's thematics also demonstrates constancy and continuity, whilst shifting its focus endlessly, often with the formal or structural rhythms, but in conformity too with the seething, available semanticity within word and world. "Polémiques I" (SB, 8-9) is a powerful example of Mitaud's bitingly sensual, sense-filled mode which spontaneously focusses social and spiritual meaning through a language forced to jump through its own aural and morphological hoops. "Le harem

79

harassé se hérisse", the poem begins, "hordes de hures ahuries / O éros orant accablé"; it then generates (self-)parodic energy as it proceeds to evoke the absent fullness that can infect language, hollow away its meanings, abusively censure and dismantle its innate cosmic and telluric pertinence. As always, however, Mitaud seeks recuperation, a transcendence of problem and polemics, firstly via a consciousness of human resistance simultaneously occurring: "il [/elle] refuse souffle efface // Le film de glaires gloses / et glas" coating self-definition; and secondly by means of an outright affirmation of will, *voyance* and sheer vitality: "veut voit vit / les sens / le sang / le sens / Nu".

Many poems merit careful discussion, but I should like especially to quote in full "Haute forêt" (SB, 24) and end by commenting briefly upon the closing text, "Art poétique" (SB, 62).

> Haute forêt d'hiver délire dénuement de la neige
> Avalanche et langage Scintillantes coulées des mots
> Branches chamarrées Déchirure Chute lente des poèmes
> Chucotement d'ailes serrées qui se déploient Essor
> D'un seul oiseau Verbe de plume et d'air
> Chant du cygne-solstice Cri de cristal
> Paroles acérées de toute lumière en décembre

This cannot be the place of a full analysis of "Haute forêt". Suffice it to say that the poem achieves great serenity whilst continuing to reveal a poetics of seething creative energy, of combative visionariness, of earthiness fused with poetic pertinence, of otherness, sheer externality, embedded into the language of self, of personal conception. "Art poétique" stresses that poetry for Mitaud is an act and a place of willed signification. Her tone is ethical and lucidly spiritual, in the term's broadest sense. Poetry rejects the prestige of its possible closure, seeks osmosis, transmission, emotive, physical and metaphysical exchange, and remains conditional on personal creative fortune. Its greatest accomplishment, far from being aesthetic, permits a simple joy, not divorced from vigilant consciousness, skipping over mortality.

Poèmes cruels (1988) is a slim *plaquette*, yet like, say, Char's *Eloge d'une Soupçonnée* of the same year, offers a remarkably condensed reading of one life's teeming array of experience--a reading, moreover, that retains a sharp but subtly aware sense of buoyancy and possibility. Thus, despite its firm articulation of motifs of bloodiness, pain, ecological violence, the soul's "hibernation" (PC, 11), the "deception" if life and the continued questioning of a language, as *Suite baroque* argued, so readily polluted or arrogantly asepticised, *Poèmes cruels* rises, through a bridging consciousness of earlier glimpsed openness, self-correction and recuperative hope, to a purer, gentler, though hard-won knowledge of existence. Here, even if tensions persist, interwoven within the poetic fabric, grace, love and mystery struggle again to their rightful expression: as Mitaud wrote at the close of *Suite baroque*, "toute déchirure devient bouche amoureuse" (SB, 57). Here she can speak of the "royalty" of existence (PC, 1) and of the "compassion of earth" (PC, 4), of the soul's unstinting affirmation and of language's deep purpose "contre un silence vénéneux" (PC, 6). Here she can give voice to her sense of the eternal freshness of being, the endless emergence of truth, absoluteness and light in their infinite manifestations. Many poems might be singled out, such as "Nuit de la Saint-Sylvestre", "Décembre", "Toute musique..." and "Dans l'herbe abâtardie..." (PC, 1, 12, 20, 28); all would show that the idea that "hors du temps règne une paix sans pleurs" (PC, 30) is not an idle one: *Poèmes cruels* is written at the intersection of a difficult alertness, a concrete compassion and an intuition of ontic and psychic depth on a cosmic scale. The transcendence it conveys is intimately rooted in seething immanence; its visions, though infinite, are real and precious.

81

Janine Mitaud's most recent publication is titled, succinctly, *Pages* (1991). This succinctness is echoed in a more abrupt articulation already hinted at, fragmented and torn half-pages being now preferred to the earlier supple, fluid continuities. A dialectics, at once affective, philosophical and aesthetic, persists amidst characteristic oppositions of aggression and love, consciousness of "ce mal sauvage et net" and a will for "forgiveness" (P, 13). Temporality is thus steadied by brief artistic "peace" and "parenthesis" (P, 10), even though it is "une poésie de fureur (P, 13) that mediates such equilibrium, a poetry hovering, Rimbaud-like, between "démence" and "un sourire de raison" (P, 23), between, too, the vigilance and divination we know to characterise Mitaud's *démarche*. A refusal to be encumbered by fear allows her poetics forever to refound itself within love's quieter maturation, within some residual, improbably ever-dawning "instant / Sans limites de lumière" (P, 18). Thus is it that her pugnacity before the crumblings and "discardedness" of existence gives way to a continuing sense of life's seemingly unlikely promise. A sobering volume, certainly, but, as "Plages" suggests, one that never loses its grip upon a yet available exhilaration:

> J'entendis le vent les vagues
> Unis
> Rompus
> Orgues cassées réaccordées
> Puis les larmes perdues dans les paroles
> Formant leur propre langage
> Primitif raffiné très secret
>
> Celui de la chair riche en prémonitions
> Celui de l'esprit qui s'arrache sans terreur
>
> Vers d'autres aires   (P, 28).

JACQUELINE RISSET

It is in 1971 that Jacqueline Risset publishes both her first critical study, *L'Anagramme du désir*, devoted to the work of Maurice Scève, and her first poetical text, the distinctly impressive, challenging and complex *Jeu*. Appearing in the Collection Tel Quel directed by Philippe Sollers, the book is arguably framed from the outset by a host of parameters that would tug it now towards a formalist or semiotic or Mallarméan rhetoric, now towards philosophical reflections à la Nietzsche, à la Spinoza, even Sartrean, now towards psychoanalytical-cum-aesthetic musings of a Lacan, a Barthes or a Derrida. Jacqueline Risset's *Jeu*, however, is never tendentious or imitative, and the "play" it at once enacts and examines as an experience, a practice and a concept, remains serious and personal, innovative and beyond gratuitousness. Divided into five parts, "Géographie (Parcours)", "Récit", "Après-récit" "Jeu" and "Méthode", the book deploys a probing, descriptive and analytical mode that, in its fragmentations, discontinuities and open, largely uncontextualised "referentiality", both queries and affirms the status, value and pertinence of its own gesture.

The first part loses no time in relating poetry to philosophy, to meditation, and argues that poetry's feasibility *and* problem lie in the contradiction of "cluttering in order to unclutter" (J,5). To write, for Risset, is to fictionally exercise and project thought: on the one hand, the text is "le récit de la vue" (J, 6), with its inner and outer poles; on the other, this *récit*, "traversing geography", becomes equally "le récit des résistances", thus pulverising perception into "des fictions... réduites à des unités minimales" (J,5). Scriptural--and contemplative-analytical--method necessarily becomes an "approximation" mimetic of the flux and uncentred interplay of the real itself

> *Tous les points sont sensibles--les fragments liés (par effacement, remplacement, développement) (développement cassé, recassé)--pas de discours admis--une méthode?*
> (J,7)

Continuity vies with piecemeal, patchwork thought, accumulations slip away into remoteness, ungraspableness, "cutting across the accumulated density" (J, 7).

The second part, titled "Récit", begins characteristically with a page that defies stable contextualisation, so that, whilst elliptically evoking the corporeal, geometric, kin(esth)etic and implicitly other relationships between some unnamed person(a)--self, other, figure in painting or photograph, etc?--and the ambient air, the sea, a table, other person(a)s, Risset's overture may well be read simultaneously as a (non-)discourse on speech or even thought in its relation to the real. Words, however, here, undoubtedly rise up so often from the vastness and the minutiae of insistently observed existence: beach, wind, dawn, birds, a stain; lines, noises, traces, surfaces; all at once in their sharpness and their cloudiness. "Toujours partir du découpage déjà fait dans ce qu'on voit", Risset notes, and although *Jeu* unquestionably moves beyond the "play" and autonomies we associate with certain *nouveau roman* approaches to seen reality, there are implicit if unelaborated affinities. The real and the textual or poetic multiply infinitely their centres; the "purpose" of their separate and yet related movements or "travels" amongst things and words is uncertain (J, 18); world and word assume a theatricalness, with "les répétitions les apparitions les disparitions" they perform (J, 17), that is not straightforwardly interpreted into fixed meaning(s). The haystacks that suddenly flash upon the poem's scene (J, 20) thus invite a reflection with proliferating parentheses which, as in Claude Simon's work, remain unclosed, i.e. open forever upon the world's/word's swarmingness. One "element" is endlessly interwoven with another (J, 21), discontinuons yet mosaical in its function, impacting upon the would-be-objective observing subject "[qui] se fai[t] traverser par ces courants variables" (J, 21) and who becomes the site, as does the poem, of a moving "idéogramme" (J, 22). The close of this second part (J, 32) emphasises the process of precarious formation and dissolution of the mosaical "object" of attention, whether it be object of vision, thought, expression or reading.

"Après-récit" begins--its opening gambit is emblematic: "--le hasard les ramène avec insistance devant nous--" (J, 35)-- by dwelling upon contradictory/complementary factors of entropy and "insistence", chance and necessity. Risset elliptically evokes the shapes and (dis)order of the world, and the "panting", rough breathing beneath, underpinning it (existentially, mentally, poetically). All is a network of lines, sounds, intentions, presences and fadings: a curious totality held between "visibility" and "invisibility". What, as philosopher-poet, Jacqueline Risset ideally seeks is what she later calls "la clef quelque part dans les croisements, dans ces rapports, à condition que rien ne soit exclu" (J, 38). She understands, too, that the "game" she plays, wedges her between a need to accept certain things, rules, to "cheat", in short, and the need to "tricher le moins possible" (J, 43) in dealing with all that "circulates", signals, passingly signifies; in dealing with the problem of the barely articulable relationships between now, non-nowness, beyond-nowness-- "maintenant nié à chaque moment par ce développement" (J, 45); in dealing with the tensions of referentiality and areferentiality (J, 45). The exquisite feasible orders imposable upon finitude are thus ceasely undermined by attention to the "interstices" (J, 58) cleaving open the latter. Risset, again like Simon, and also Michel Deguy, can render concrete these infinitely shifting interpretive interstices by insisting upon alternatives, parallel (conceptual) structure, by multiplying metamorphoses/metaphors, again like Simon or Michel Deguy: "LE BRUIT TOUCHE LA FORME // aussi bien se développant l'un à côté de l'autre, ou se rencontrant ou passant d'un point à un autre ou changeant" (J, 63). The elusive, somehow hidden (inter)pertinence of (present) phenomena thus collides with the pressing feeling that "la source [est] proche néanmoins (ici)" (J, 64) and Risset's "response" plunges her into the kind of intricate half-Mallarméan, half-early-Robbe-Grilletian elaboration that closes off--but without really closing it--the *jeu* of "Après-récit" (J, 70).

The fourth part, "Jeu", written under the sign of Wittgenstein as elsewhere, stresses from the outset the infinite flexibility of the part in relation to all other (visible/imaginable) parts, but adds that what is seen, the "vision", is understood now to be nothing else than "le jeu lui-même son développement clair et calme" (J, 75). In this game of "dice" and movement, however, what still orients Risset's eye, mind and hand, is the structure of the things of the world, "les détails, l'ensemble / les rapports vus, décrits" (J, 91); or, for example, "ce qui dans l'image... a la fonction exacte: 'rivière'" (J, 78). Hereness, the *hic et nunc* with all its enigmas, "ce qui s'intitule de soi-même, à tort mais irréprochablement: 'ici'" (J, 77): this is what remains at the centreless, uncentrable centre of Jacqueline Risset's *jeu/Jeu* that seeks finally to traverse it, rather circumscribe it--though even this traversal should be understood to be non-linear, just as its "objects" are circulating, bubbling, birthing-dying-(re)forming, present-passing: "Devant les yeux dissolution / Ni là ni-- // Sécrété par le tout: sans ligne" (J, 100). Faced with all of this, *Jeu* offers "[une] réponse interrogeante" (J, 107) and its inscription is founded upon a "presqu'unique devoir: le soupçon permanent. Et la gaîté presqu'aveugle" (J, 105). The latter element, of course, releases poetry, and thought, from a kind of functional anxiety into which "serious reflection" and inscription could so easily slide. The "continuous trembling" to which "beaches, forests, cities, objects displaced and replaced" (J, 114) are subjected via language, is thus not a sign of deep anguish. The word's trembling comes from its ever-thrusting motion, its mingling action, its disordering and reordering, the intentional and unintended movements provoked, the bustling "equality" it establishes for itself and for the phenomena it spectrally represents (cf. J, 111).

The final part of *Jeu*, "Méthode,", begins by quoting a thought from Lao-Tzu which, to say the least, complicates the notions of (non-)centre and play already elaborated, seemingly turning them about upon themselves. "Animer le jeu droit au centre et hors-jeu"... But, of course, in *Jeu*, in the (inter)play of world and thought and word, everything is and isn't a centre, and there are no rules: off-sides can hardly apply in a game where traversal is not really spatial (cf. J, 147). "Toute agglomération, foculation, mûrissement" is thus immersed in a logic, a sense, a plurality (J, 133); the networking of relationships creates double, triple, no doubt even infinite, "knots" between "*là, et là*" (J, 141). Observation, description, articulation, "c'est la sortie des évidences, affleurement de blocs fragmentés, ordres disparaissant dans leur énonciation, satisfaction, écume" (J, 149). The "method" Jacqueline Risset has at various moments and again here in a classic passage (J, 132) evoked, the turning and churning it generates, not surprisingly lead to what she varyingly calls "froth"--we are between Mallarmé and Bonnefoy--and play, "*comme, comme si*" (J, 155): "ni résultat, ni non-résultat, ni entre les deux / --

87

sinon ce qui serait 'entente' entre les deux" (J, 151). A "nothingness", a "dissolving arisen in one's hands" (J, 157).

Seven years after this demanding and searching poetic debut appears the no less complex, though perhaps at times--I think in particular of the book's final section bearing the volume's title--less efficacious *La Traduction commence* (1976). Published with Bourgois in the collection directed by Bénézet and Lacoue-Barthe, it is predicated at once upon the doubt and the necessity clinging to the scriptural, though presumably that "near-blind gaiety" espoused in the poetics of *Jeu* may be embedded in this necessity. Four parts order--illusionistically, no doubt, but also in a gesture of combative conceptualism--the book. The first, "Corpus (histoire)", seems to focus, via ellipses much more striking than in *Jeu*, upon the (mental and textual) "order" beyond objects yet dipping into their infinite potential, the transformational-conceptual fragmentation and reworking that they occasion for the poet-philosopher. "Une loi fausse de succession" (TC, 16) is at once what this "order" generates and seeks to flee or, at minimum, interrogate via its very creation. The non-place, non-time of this order, the derisoriness or "funniness" of its (dis)continuities are thus treated to a poetic "creusement successif, simultané, progressif" (TC, 28) that, literally, hollow and "perforate" poetic/perceptual fullness, showing the text or poem to be the text-as-memory-as-oblivion (cf. TC, 28). All figuration, in this perspective, can be no more than "légère figure" (TC, 32), but, by the same perverse but reassuring token, failure provides new option: "la fête, étant manquée, peut commencer" (TC, 32).

"Cor (discours)" is the title of the book's second section, which again, via the doubling of the parenthesis, functions in an enigmatic, symbolic (*sum-ballein*, cast-together), meta-morphic/metaphoric mode. Affirmation and suspicion cohabit--we might think of Char, Jabès, even

88

Bonnefoy, as well as Teyssiéras, Etienne and Le Dantec in their different ways; the anti-discourse bursts open, turns the "woof" inside out and breaks its own "threads" (cf. TC, 39); a "flapping" rhythm of "outside inside" develops; flow and slippage result without precise end ("ainsi vers quoi", TC, 46). But this abyssal dis-array and di-splay/dis-play, this work as mere "as-ness" ("'Que mon travail--Comme'" (TC, 50), offers, in its very breaking, and as with a poet such as Jaccottet, a "shining", a gleaming, a flashing illumination in inverted commas, that somehow renders the whole more necessary than dubious.

"Timor (rouge)" and "La Traduction commence" are the titles, respectively, of the third and final parts of this exploded-imploded collection. The myth of Pasiphae floats loosely over the third part, with its factors of blind and strange love, its connection with concepts of labyrinth and delicately "threaded" solution (Daedalus and Ariadne), madness and transgenericalness (Phaedra and Minotaur). Fear and death play their skeletal roles also, but always silhouetted against a backcloth of vertigo, tense laughter and a "redness" which would seem to lie somewhere between that of a Denis Roche (*Le Mécrit, Louve basse*, etc.) and that of an Yves Bonnefoy (*Le Nuage rouge, La Vie errante*): that is to say, somewhere in the vicinity of what Risset calls "le hasard, le soudain" (TC, 66), and, although meditated, more flagrantly raw, wild, spontaneous and elliptical than, "*pendant des milliers d'années, toutes les méthodes*", and even her own of *Jeu*. The instability of all meaning and relationship is not surprisingly implied and indeed constantly enacted-- "que veut dire ceci, que je te / que nous nous", we read, for example, at the threshold of "Timor (rouge)"--and, although such non-knowing, tension and contradiction ("oui et non à l'intérieur des organes") can generate some exhilaration, there is, one feels, a certain fear of self-

89

dissolution in the "riant/éloignement" Risset's work traverses (TC, 76). Insistency and dispersal are in taut complementarity in this direly fragmented saga of Language and Eros (cf. back cover). "Quelque chose va être trouvé / mais déjà vidé //.../ torsion de l'esprit qui lui fait plaisir" (TC, 76). The closing "La Traduction commence" may "bear up the texts" (ibid.) of Yi King, Scève, Proust, Lucretius (*De rerum natura*) and Joyce, but the lacunae are vast, the loss considerable, the creative residue hanging by a few threads--all so consciously so.

It is not until 1985, although after long, painstaking work on Dante, that Jacqueline Risset's *Sept passages de la vie d'une femme* appears. If inevitably close to the earlier poetical work in certain ways, it is a book that the poet herself knows to be in other ways sensibly different. "Il faut qu'il y ait coupure pour qu'il y ait le chant", she tells us. "Musique amnésique; chant rapide, danse, passage des danseuses. *Voyage, vision, rêve, transe...* Autres pays, autres gestes, découpage par le hasard et montage par l'artisan appliqué // Temps d'absolu de la sensation, vérité atteinte? et disparaissant // Centre du monde, à présent éclaté, vide--l'insensé, explosion du dérèglement" (back cover). The essential continuities in Risset's poetics are well pinpointed: rupture, oblivion, presence-as-absence, Rimbaldian "dancing", traversal, chance and mental-cum-aesthetic moulding, multiplication, the tensions of the absolute and of dispersal, void, *dérèglement*, and so on. The new collection, however, performs so urgently, so directly, the poetics of rupture and becoming that we find ourselves in a textual environment which has undergone--as will that of *L'Amour de loin* and, again, *Petits éléments de physique amoureuse*--significant modal and hence conceptual changes. "Screen-memory" (SP, 9) is the opening poem of the first of no less than seventeen sections or suites composing the collection. Written in

90

an unpunctuated continuous prose like all seven of the liminal "Sept passages de la vie d'une femme", and in this unlike all the other sixteen varyingly orchestrated free-verse sections, the poem compactly voices uncontextualised yet insistent primary experience, at once visualised and half-screened-out, probably of childhood, perhaps infancy, an experience caught in its mystery, its sensuality, the open reflection to which it submits, the conceptual-aesthetic framing of its opening and terminal gambits.

Let me invite now a reading of another "first" poem, this time of the third section, "Fragments arrachés à la philosophie", and titled "Lettre brûlée" (SP, 27):

> ceci, le fait en vérité qu'il ne faut pas
> craindre le poids de la terre par rapport
> à son état de suspendue
> vide--et à la fois
> lieu qui permet le passage
> nature subtile
> par le moyen de la vue à la nuit, ou bien
> quelque sensation conservée
> dans l'âme
> et s'avançant vers une
> mesure de surgissement
> et de la disparition
> savoir les différences
> par l'infini dans les rapports
>
> et l'affirmation, imparfaite.

What might be most usefully stressed, initially, is Risset's sense of our travelling and traversal of the earth as not just sensory and physical, nor exclusively conceptual, mental or philosophical: from *Sept passages de la vie d'une femme* on, the spiritual, affective and meta-physical dimensions of experience are given increasing weight. The notions--and sensations--of emergence and fading, finitude and infinity, "affirmation" and mortality

91

(that Bonnefidian "imperfection [qui] est la cime") all speak, in that elegant halting style, of an impact of things upon the self so deep as to transcend any banal phenomenological reduction. In this sense the poem feeds back into the earlier "Des pays étranges" and "Enigme" (SP, 12, 15); it hints again at that feeling of utter astonishment before our "being-here" (SP, 14), or the stupefaction of all creativity/createdness (SP, 11); the precarious lightness of all ontic passingness, all "being Fire and smoke in the blackness" (SP, 15, 23).

It would be wonderful, in similar fashion, to mull over the subtle fragments of the long "Dans la barque / Dorata" (SP, 39-46) or the surging kaleidoscopic stanzas of "Indostan" (SP, 107-112). These and other poems would all tell, and tell of, the sheer forcefulness and the mere trace of experience via poetry. They would sing its play and its oblivion, its intense colouring and its passing, its nothingness. They would show, as does poem III of "9 poèmes de Mnémosyne" (SP, 52), that the equations of time and space are in flux, perhaps delusional despite our best efforts. The *élan* of poetry, and of life itself, may bear us up, may offer affirmation and "transport"; but the "gloria gloria" remains bracketted to "Wort oubli", as poem VI of the same above suite concludes (SP, 56). "Ainsi", Risset argues, like some latter-day Lamartine in her "Eté à la fenêtre à Rome", "dans la même phrase on y croit et on n'y croit plus / tout le parcours de l'illusion est parcouru en une seule phrase" (SP, 65). And, here we have perhaps a clear glimpse of that elusive--non-existent!--non-centre of her poetics: the triangular struggle between the will to comprehend, the tensions of (non-)belief, and the imperious injunction of her gaze upon the world about her and the resultant "amour absolu de tout objet / qui meurt" (SP, 66). The closing poem of the collection, "Paradisiaca XXXIII" (SP, 119-23) is too long to quote here.

Its richly but raggedly woven text conjures many images, notions and experiences and is run through with intertextual or aesthetically self-reflexive fragments. What seems most pressing is the question/experience of joy, "petite" or "paradisiaca", "divine" or simply "douceur", bookish, purely aesthetic or intimately bound up with time, mortality, grass, "bruit de fontaine", "cri d'oiseau enfoncé dans mémoire". Syntactic and semantico-referential ellipses break up the poem but open it to our invited access. The "stifling" or emotional choking that is evoked on a number of occasions can be linked to Mallarmé, Valvins, his obsession with *le Livre*, the death of his eight-year-old son so painfully commemorated in (Jean-Pierre Richard's) *Pour un tombeau d'Anatole*. Or it can--perhaps via the same allusion--be anchored in the visceral experience of simple, ephemeral and exquisitely mortal things:

> ah divine émotion instants arrachés à la trame
> ah lutter avec l'herbe et l'herbage
> fraîche d'indicible arraché
> à ces lieux à ton corps-coeur.

Mallarmé certainly haunts the poem, but the latter leaps beyond overt specificity, bathing all in its moving path--"*Lavato nell'acqua di poesia*", is its opening line--, giving to each fragment as to each moment lived, "exhausted" yet "swarming", the beauty and the fragileness of its miracle, "coup d'ineffable ah sentence de sibylle".

The 1988 *L'Amour de loin* has been preceded, in the interval since the publication of *Sept passages de la vie d'une femme*, by translations of Dante and Fellini and by a critical study of the work of Marcelin Pleynet. Its epigraph, from Guillaume de Poitiers, reaffirms the insubstantial, "voided", purely symbolic nature of the poetic, and the literary in general: its "inventedness"--yet an inventedness that, despite apparent denial to the contrary, relates urgently to what it no longer quite is nor can be: the

93

teeming vibrancy of life itself. This "poème de rien pur", then, may be reduced to a strictly symbolic homological relation to the lived, but there is no doubt that this relation is crucial to the writing and the reading of *L'Amour de loin*, a doubly telling title, speaking of aesthetic remoteness and affective becoming and rhythmic constancy. The book is organised into five sections moving from "Printemps" to "Printemps" and, although the course charted of the intimacy and love between the collection's *je* and *tu* shows those myriad symptoms well characterised by Risset's predecessors such as Pernette du Guillet, Louise Labé, Madame de Lafayette and Marceline Desbordes-Valmore (cf. "Les Phénomènes d'amour", AL, 30-31, and "Des inconvénients et petits accidents d'amour", AL, 89-90), the book also seeks to stress the pertinence of such love to a more broadly experienced love, a love of, and reciprocated by, the world at large, that we have seen Jacqueline Risset's work constantly articulate:

> flamme d'un arbre, vite
> choc d'une rivière, ou d'une eau calme
> faisant signe au détour
>   par regard
> comme amour   (AL, 21).

Shifting, kaleidoscopic emotions and perceptions, changing expression of changing states, love's niceties, depths and enigmas, its capacity to have us see a sacredness at the heart of all experience, a "halo" around all being (AL, 25)--these are the elements that dominate and proliferate in Risset's current poetics. Love, whatever its nature and object, is seen as "surging forth... / absolute / trembling" (AL, 22); its logic is overpowering, inexplicable, but felt--if anything ever is in Risset--to be central; it is based in the sensory, but "goes down to the heart / ... trying us / and perfecting us" (AL, 25) in a spiral of ethical and spiritual maturation. Love, moreover, spreads this contagion: its object, its "name", "ce toi rend tout visible / tout frais", giving to the face of all others the face of the beloved,

> visage glissé dans [l]a matière
> pour l'animer la faire saisir
> --autrement morte, inerte:
>
> > ocre battant
> > respirant   (AL, 29).

Thus does Risset's *corps-coeur*, of "Paradisiaca XXXIII" and again here of "Amor che ne la mente" (AL, 36-7), find near-synonymy with the "soul" in a conception of love linking it to the harmonies and (a)rhythmic paradisiacal order of some music of the spheres, "amour qui résonne / qui raisonne //... / Amour qui me fais penser / et me dévies toutes mes pensées" (AL, 36).

Such experience, shattering thought as it forms it, radically problematises its own expression. The *poiesis* that would capture love thus constitutes no more--though no less: Risset loops round to her epigraphic pronouncement--than "[une] grande approximation des mots du poème: / ils chantent / ils figent // en velours et poussière" (AL, 41). Dusty nothingness and velvety beauty...; "odeur de présent dans le vide" (AL, 51). Just as writing may be perceived as celebratory, commemorative, an act of guardianship, so may it seem to compound, even induce separation, the *acqua di poesia* "bathes me no more" (AL, 95). In this, moreover, it reflects the antipodal feelings traversing the self, as well as the general cyclical, "seasonal" shifts *L'Amour de loin* performs; but its "dissolution des phrases / arbres" (AL, 94) may originate on the "outside" with the other, although Risset, as we have already seen in *Sept passages de la vie d'une femme*, rightly deconstructs simplistic inside-outside dichotomies, just as the opening text of *L'Amour de loin* refuses to embrace quick

95

categories of temporality and their accompanying logic of origin, cause and effect: "mais il n'y a pas de premier moment" (AL, 11). The lessons of the heart, and of language's attachment to them, are in effect more subtle and elusive than reductive intellectualism would allow. Love possesses, unanalysed, its own intelligence, which lies, anguish or ecstasy, in its vast experience. "Tout lui sert, chaque être, chaque paysage", the collection concludes (AL, 106). The mystery love traverses may barely be comprehended, but it *is* known, because lived. "L'Hiver" puts it this way:

> l'amour est donc ceci:
> imperceptible trait
> de montée qui demande?
>
> intonation de demande étonnée
> où tout s'engouffre
> mince intervalle
>
> disant:
> tout change
> toutes cellules remuées
>
> > :une voyelle
> > dite un peu plus haut dans la voix--
> > un souffle--
> > (AL, 98).

The experience and the poetics of love continue to preoccupy Jacqueline Risset in her most recent and delicately woven *Petits éléments de physique amoureuse* (1991). We are far, here, from some banal catalogue of purely physical options and adventures. The deep ontic significance of love is at stake, its generalised relevance, the half-forgotten, largely "invisible" meaning of a "physics" intricately psychological, spiritual, tied to the minutiae of fleeting instants, "[ce] rien / qui est le tout // [cette] allégresse à ce droit de dire / : 'tout'" (PE, 114). In this optic the artistic or poetic gesture is always a gesture of love caught up at once in the high specificity of personal experience and a

96

sense of mythical recognition, honouring, consecration even, of the this-ness of life, yet, beyond, of something more "distant", more essential, more originary, cosmic: "énergie éternel délice" (PE, 19). The love of which Risset speaks, in her still finely elliptical but subtly allusive and oddly limpid style, is thus a phenomenon that is multiple, infinite, within the self's becoming ephemeralness and quiddity, yet ever-nascent, spurting forth from seeming "nothingness", feeding upon all--flowers, sounds, fragrance, forms, emotions, words--that constantly floods before and through us as otherness, as the *tu* of existence, the unspoken yet now-speaking silence of being's instants, instances, *instances*, of alterity. Gazing, waiting, writing thus permit an endless experience of *reconnaissance*--discovery and gratitude--, of the possibility of speaking as *we*, of knowing the depth of visceral and psychic pertinence of "everything", of the urgency and joy of each "vif instant de naissance absolue" (PE, 58). Large questions of identity, of being and having, of presence and absence, become rethinkable in the light of what Jacqueline Risset's prefatory essay calls "l'amour de la poésie" (PE, 7). One thinks of Jacques Roubaud and one is tempted--but the matter is irrelevant, swept away by Risset's own *conversation souveraine*--to polemically oppose her poetics to that *haine de la poésie* of which Bataille, Noël and Roche have spoken. I prefer to conclude by offering some compact appreciation of a handful of poems.

The first, untitled, from "Le Feu", the third of the book's twelve sections, can be quoted:

> Instant présent
>
> qui passe
>
> dans cet air-ci cette fumée
>
> brillant   (PE, 40).

Shorter by far than all but one or two of the collection's texts, the poem proceeds like a Guillevician *quantum* or one of Jaccottet's earlier *airs*, and is a perfect example of those *petits éléments* or *éclats* (PE, 10) that textually mime the experience they relate at the intersection of minimality and some maximum. Presence, whilst slipping ineluctably away in some invisible temporal drift through the very atmosphere in which our being bathes, also "passes", transmutes, into that other this-ness or specificity that is poetry, *cet air-ci* and no other. Smoke, as Bonnefoy and Jaccottet and others have equally termed both the primary and the metaphoric or symbolic passage, it nevertheless succeeds--*éclat* in its otherness--in flashing before and within us its inalienable brilliance, its double lightedness.

"Odeur de fleur ce matin..." (PE, 45) is the first of three texts composing the fourth section which takes its title from its liminal poem. All three are, in effect, linked and could be read as one, the first opening out upon the second via an unclosed punctuation: this, of course, should be borne in mind to the extent that it would extend the brief observations I offer. The use of the unrhymed (or rather occasionally, only accidentally rhymed) free-verse three-line stanza provides added continuity and the line-length, going from 4 to 15 syllables but "centred" upon a decasyllabic structure, confirms this instinct of coherence and equilibrium. The point of departure is the simple, the quotidian and the sensory, at once finite ("ce matin") and essential ("odeur": not *une odeur*); and what follows, "dans la vie suspendue seul transport est l'amour--/ transport d'amour", seems to set up a dialectics mirroring this tension (suspendedness and movement), whilst thereby emphasising the degree to which love is felt to be the prime moving force, the motor of ecstasy (ec-stasy). "Oui: comme un camion qui vous fait sortir" begins the second stanza, developing

98

Risset's rhetoric of affirmation (beyond the somewhat fading "suspicion" of the earlier poetics), living easily the *comme/comme si* of her speech (the poetics of metaphor/metamorphosis-as/*transport d'amour*: "l'amour de la poésie") as well as the logic that underpins it (experience acts through language to "throw one / [in]directly into the noise [of life] into the heart")--into an inside-outside now "transported", ec-stas. All of this, moreover, is actualised via an amplification of the "instant": an expansion or infinitisation of the apparently finite whereby "cet instant est coeur du monde", opening nowness to its avatars, opening the self to its other, (its) love, (its) transportability. The closing stanza (with its suspended comma, I stress again) returns us to a sense of the minimality of all of this, that remains yet *ma vie*, irreplaceable, ineffable, infinitely centred centre of endless such *jeux*:

> ceci n'est que ma vie, prise en un point,
> se regardant, regardant rien, peut-être pas même toi,
> qui seulement étais là, à ce moment-là,

Such a fragment or *éclat*--as is the experience, as is the poem--gazes upon itself both as fullness (*ma vie*) and nothingness (*rien, peut-être pas même toi*), sensing in combined event something, some meaning exceeding its signs, "merely" to be lived, fragmentedly voiced, yet joyously traversed as the act and the symbol of *transport d'amour*.

The final poem to which I wish to draw attention opens the tenth section entitled "Pentecôte".

> Je suis là devant l'air
> soleil naissant façade lisse
> cris perçants d'hirondelles
> légers parcours croisés
> rythme

parfait moment reconnaissable
où l'attente
--de quoi?
est à elle seule
--rien de précis mais la présence--
joie et aussi
joie-certitude   (PE, 97).

Poem of simple being-there, of being with, *devant*, at once witness and participant, this short text with its freely disciplined metric orchestration (6, 8, 6, 6, 1 + 8, 3 + 2, 5, 8, 4 + 4) moves from an insistence upon external factors, relationships, networks, rhythm(s), to a reflection upon the psychological, emotional and implicitly spiritual pertinence of such "external" parameters. The seeing and the hearing meld with a "recognition" that has nothing of the banally intellectual about it: it is a discovery that relies not upon surface assessment (*rien de précis*) but honours rather the depth of lived, livable emotion, ec-stasy, that passing, slowly or quickly metamorphosing instants can bring--given an availability that avoids firm expectation (as to knowledge, meaning, purpose, etc.). To attain to such "recognition", unscientific, unrepeatable in the same terms, is to attain to a release, a liberation, of emotion that, paradoxically, instead of casting Risset adrift upon the seas of anxiety and doubt, allows access to a certainty owing nothing to analysis, all to consent.

ANNE TEYSSIÉRAS

The work of Anne Teyssiéras, from her 1966 *Epervier ma solitude* to her most recent *Le Chemin sous la mer* (1992) shows a remarkable concentration of emotional and psychological energy caught within discreetly modulated poetic forms hesitating between the visionary and the hyperconscious. The image of the sparrow-hawk in the title of *Epervier ma solitude*, and taken up in one of the closing texts, "Solitude" (ES, np), would seem to suggest a level of dynamism and vigorous seizure associated with solitary action that Paul Chaulot's perceptive preface somewhat understates. Struck by Teyssiéras' "tormented [but stubborn] approach to the real", he stresses rather the slippery, evasive nature of objects of observation and desire, their *leurre*, the silence and the void guarding their access. The ascetic, bare strategies he perceives in this early work may constitute a strength, but they leave a "taste of ash", moving, though eloquent of a "vulnerability".

Much of *Epervier ma solitude* obeys these shrewdly caught nuances. Take, for example, "Liberté", the opening poem:

> Ma cage est une main de jardinier sans île
> où pousse l'âge obscur
> sans égard aux bêtes à venir
>
> Ma cage est le rayon d'une étoile aquatique
> qui m'a touchée du mal
> de naître et de mourir.   (ES, np)

We are seemingly far from Eluard's poems of freedom. All appears ironic; liberty is defined in terms of imprisonment and, although the latter offers some seeming compensation (cage as a "gardener's hand" and watery starlight), strange additional ironies spiral experience down into absence, obscurity and disregard, the double malady of life and death.

And the volume's second poem, "Origine", does little, arguably, to lighten a burden weighing firmly upon Teyssiéras' early poetic consciousness: loss, unknowing, shadowiness of the other's presence, the "illegibility" of the self's hands, original, primal laceration and blinding of the self, exclusion or, at best, minimal, vestigial contact... And yet, even here, in these two poems, a poetics of *conceivable* liberation remains; questioning and desire *are* powerful agents of discovery; residual availability is not synonymous with nothingness. Thus is it that a poem like "sommeil" can evoke the plusses and the minusses of being; that the incapacity and inexperience of "Terrain vague" or the dearth and absence "decipher[able] / in the hollow of our hands" (cf. "Routes sans merci") may be said to reach a fragile equilibrium with lived principles of innocence and love, freshness and universal contact (cf. "Chardons"). Certainly, the hawkish claw of solitude has written its harsh "ciphers" upon "mes fleurs mes étapes", and escape seems to be boxed in "sous les mirages clos". But, to my mind, and despite its sadness and marked sobriety, "L'Epave", the lushly rhythmed closing poem of the volume, demonstrates that Anne Teyssiéras' experiences--of death, consequent abandonment and "wreckage"--are far from submerging her traumatically. There remains, indeed emerges, here, a softness, a tender caressing of the painful yet exquisite mystery of incarnation and passing that allow one to speak of a paradoxical reenergising of the self in the vastly increased complexity of its assumed relationship with the real. Respect, contemplative penetration of experience, a sense of love remarkably transcendent of vicissitude: these are, finally, determining factors in this budding poetics.

The 1969 *Fragments pour une captive* continues to explore these tensions and bare equilibriums of *Epervier ma solitude*. The new collection develops a rhetoric less of the ambivalence or wilful paradox than of the sensed and lived interpenetration of factors of imprisonment and deliverance, absence and presence, darkness and source-light. All centres upon a traumatising and yet reenergising experience of loss: loss of the other, of the other woman, of mother, source, origin, of an incompletely understood and unresolved psychological gestalt at once problematic and deeply, frustratingly possible. A feeling of the grievous impotence of definitive separation combines from the outset with a continued expectation, a thought of still feasible knowing, a "raising of the shroud" now (FC, 7) and an oddly effortless "bearing up" of the lost other (FC, 8). Interestingly, and crucially, what emerges from this "absence [qui] est mon intime déchirure" (FC, 11)--from a *fêlure* that, seemingly, had already existed, moreover, a cleft or loss before the cleft of present loss--is a present and future action (: the poetic gesture) which, at least occasionally, appears capable of healing and joining:

> Je chanterai l'eau primitive -- celle qui jaillit des solitudes de l'argile, en gerbes froides.
>
> J'irai renouant les climats divisés dans la prunelle du soleil.   (FC, 12)

Teyssiéras' is a poetry at once of confession and blind seeing. It hovers between revolt and tenderness, pain and freshness. Its "fragments" struggle to cohere, both opaquely impetuous, visceral *cris*, and yet transparent in their immediacy and their obsessiveness. *Tombeaux* in the double way Mallarmé's work could be--via poetic transcendence, but also, as intense and deeply tense works such as *Hérodiade, Igitur* or the exquisite *Tombeau pour Anatole* Jean-Pierre Richard has offered us--Anne Teyssiéras' caressed fragments permit an improbable creative radiation-- "telle qu'en moi-même devenue l'éblouissement de ta mort" (FC, 31)--

103

where "our alliance" seemed irrevocably "lost" (F, 34). Such a creation may allow the self to arise from a mutual *déroute* and the self's own "thickness" (FC, 35), but Teyssiéras is equally conscious, at this early stage and increasingly, of dangers of a poetics of "tombality": incapacity, immobility, obsession and so on. "Serai-je bien un jour cette chose de toi dévorée par des oiseaux?", she asks (FC, 38). And is not the "captive" of the title the subject as well as the object of *poiesis*? And "building" accomplished is thus instinctively felt to have to be provisional and symbolic, beyond the visceral. "Je bâtirai", she writes, somewhat à la Bonnefoy, "des jours de sable, soleil et pluie, hors de nous" (FC, 38); *Fragments pour une captive* is an accomplished though ephemeral gesture of painful yet needed funereal singing. Its aim is no doubt release, but, discreet and solemn as it is, it remains caught in a clinging web of complex, still unreleased emotion.

Cinq étapes pour une attente (1971) pursues similar formal strategies to those found in *Fragments pour une captive*: compact prose texts, usually orchestrated into two or three short *strophes* or paragraphs. No indentation occurs, however, nor are there entire italicised texts, and punctuation, sparse but present before, now almost completely disappears. All is discreet yet focussed, centred, just as, modally, urgency balances restraint, and darting metaphor melds with elision, non-contextualisation, a purity of *signifiance*. The opening poem, untitled like all the others, develops what seems to be a double logic of "all love at the approach of evening" (CE, 2): on the one hand "ce bruit de baisers au vol des hirondelles", a symbolics of lightly brushing soft caress, and on the other hand "partout l'étendue des sables recouverts / tant de fois meurtrière à l'appel endeuillé d'une / mouette" (CE, 1), a symbolics now of melancholia, barrenness, mourning and intrinsic cosmic violence. Within

104

this tautness of metaphorised emotion, waiting allows for survival, "son désir rougeoie contre les portes closes" CE, 5), and we assume that such passive or active questing (cf. CE, 6) could just possibly lead to a synthesis of the elements of the logic of love and certainly to, at least, a transcendence of the rumbling, stumbling, shuddering sense of abandonment, of *le presque-rien*, that "Elle dit dans le parcours..." (CE, 19) evokes. Poetry, here, appears to match the intransitiveness, the imprisoning, self-encircling closure of existential effort: "un geste d'adoration qui ne pouvait s'achever qu'en lui-même" (CE, 24). And, indeed, one feels that Teyssiéras is again, but differently, grappling in this volume with the paradoxes of her very poetic action: the pull of alterity, self-transcendence, the perils of closure, yet the need to look within for psychic coherence, the possibility that "nothing may happen" from the outside in (CE, 25). The beautiful penultimate text spells out these tensions as it begins by announcing:

Ici il n'y a rien mais tout   (CE, 29).

And the collection's final poem points to the "truth" of fire (CE, 30): its consumption of all, the ephemerality and provisionality of our ontic and poetic traversal of self, and of the other.

Dedicated "to my mother", the 1974 *Dernier état* picks up on this notion of passage and extinction as its liminal poem declares with its characteristically preferred water imagery: "La vague efface la vague" (DE, 2). Such a notion of erasure, however, does not deny gathering; rather does it tie the latter to a poetics of endless repetition, rhythmic, fragmented recommencement, "pareil au raclement de l'eau sur les cailloux / le souffle intermittent" (DE, 4). Such rhythms manifestly may dovetail with Teyssiéras' logic of waiting and expectation, but it is clear, too, that she understands the degree to which such poetico-existential

105

action is caught up in an aporetic rhetoric of ghostliness and presence, silence and speech, semantic bewilderment (: "il n'y a pas de grille absolue contre l'égarement des signes" DE, 20) and deep meaning: "J'exhausse à contre-jour des gestes sans échos", she can write (DE, 7), or, elsewhere, speak of "*une pensée qui / écarte ce qu'elle désigne*" and "ton silence [qui] fut mon séjour" (DE, 8). Being-there and disappearance thus constantly fuse their difference into some impalpable yet experienced *différance*. The intransitiveness of the ontic experience--"car toujours plus absente et là" (DE, 12)--thus mirrors/is mirrored by the non-attainment (: repetition, wave-like recommencement) of all poetic practice. The vaguely hallucinatory, half-visionary quality of these poems no doubt corresponds to such factors, for the poetico-ontic seeing Teyssiéras seeks to engender is ever problematised by the very nature and circumstances of her task: "comment remédier aveugle à cette grande déperdition", she asks (DE, 24), knowing yet that the "fire" of being never eradicates the love that peers through it (cf. DE, 30).

The next five years, 1975-79, see a dense flurry of collections published, all pressing further forward into the mushrooming intricacies of factors already elaborated. *L'Ecaille des eaux* (1975) is the first of these collections and exploits in a much more conspicuous manner the counterpoint of roman and italic representation of voice. The mode is still obsessive and that of some psychological yet equally metaphysical hothouse, but we are at once far from sheer esotericism and yet in a world seeking serenity and distance within the intimacy and intensity of focus. Written under the sign of an Artaud speaking of the absolute's questing after the relative, the volume offers thirty simply numbered poems "arranged" under three arguably progressive--or cyclical, repetitive, "oceanic" as Hugo or Lautréamont might say--headings: "Rencontre",

"Eclipse", "Regain". The opening poem seems to have developed greater distance from the emotions surrounding death and appreciates that this distance does not proscribe a simple caring for the other, an "encounter" essentially on and in the self's, the survivor's, terms. Poem IX, from the "Eclipse" suite, confirms that current encounter is at ease with disappearance, finitude and finality, yet recognises that "*il faut encore libérer ces quelques cris de bête enfouis dans l'épaisseur de sa mémoire*". That such liberation is essentially the self's need hardly be stressed, nor that the "eye which sees [at the bottom of a pit]" belongs to the half-blind, half-glimpsing poet. The closing poem XXX is brief but eloquent of Teyssiéras' becoming perception:

> Son visage a grandi sous une clarté d'eau
> Le bruissement des feuilles en aggrave la solitude
> Ainsi voit-on naître la terre
> Et la mort n'est plus qu'une porte en ruines

Drowning, disappearance and solitariness do not disallow images of magnification and the implicit *magnificat* it contains. And it seems characteristic of the poems of "Regain" that death is oddly reduced to rubble--the image remains of course ambivalent, but its paradox suggests access, unblocking, and not a merely confirmed collapse--and that, most tellingly, birth, rebirth dominates imaginatively.

The opening text of the 1976 *Parallèles* pursues this poetics of (re-)generation and reminds us of the fundamentally intertextual, self-citational and interwoven character of Anne Teyssiéras' poetic *œuvre*. Any burial of the old cry or "song... of the long solitudes" (P, 7) thus is synonymous with newly emergent voice. The volume's title, of course, with the epigraph accompanying it, also speaks of a *parole imprononçable* imaginable at a point of convergence of separate discourses--and even somehow, perhaps, realised, as poetic voice slips through the hoops of its own becoming? Once more loss is thus imbricated with phantasmal presence, visceral intensity with more serene distance, and the counterpoint of roman and italicised print concretises such imbrication. "Son nom aigu comme l'écharde a traversé / ma langue" (P, 17), Teyssiéras affirms, stressing the decussation of different nominations, languages, voices of being. The poem "L'Une et l'autre parallèles..." (P, 19), not dissimilarly, articulates, via an italicised voice already complicating the volume's discourse, an intricate thematics of separation and similitude, doubling within doubling, cross-purposes and interference, love and absolute distinction. Such "écriture fulgurante", as another text terms it (P, 26), is at once brilliant and blinding, broken and whole, caught between anxiety and a "joy... slow to scatter / the remains of the flotsam" (P, 26). Such joy, such slowly assumed simplicity of love, resides, still for the moment, perhaps is destined to ever reside, within the paradox, the tensional flow of a movement that, on the one hand, sheds mourning, exile, the rhetoric of "swampedness", for "ailleurs me somme" (P, 32); and, on the other hand, propels the self towards the other, its traps, *tombeaux* and mirage-like guardianship (P, 36).

Lest we be tempted to believe the trials and tribulations of Anne Teyssiéras' poetic self-voicing to be resolved, or about to be transcended, *Le Pays d'où j'irai* of 1977 sharply reaffirms the intensity of her continuing struggle. Images of death, poison, pallor, ennui and destruction abound. "La chute commence où finit l'élan", she writes, seemingly confirming a regression to earlier incapacity, or, possibly, an accession to a new existential, and consequently poetic, problematics stemming, perhaps, from the very accommodations already slowly achieved. Whatever the unspecified source of crisis, metaphors of contortion, distortion, rotting, disconnectedness and *agonie* prevail (LP, 11). Life becomes a non-place of insomnia, fatal introversion, just as language associates itself with feelings of lassitude, non-existence and nausea. As with Beckett, and perhaps with a similar poetics of derision, if we are to believe the later reflections of *Les Clavicules de Minho*, great cosmic and inner activity does not modify her sense that "nothing is happening" (LP, 16), that

> C'est un paysage de sable impossible
> à redresser
> Le sang s'infiltre sous les grains
> fade ruissellement
> où s'épuise à prendre congé
> une voix devenue blanche   (LP, 20).

It is essential, however, not to lose sight of the implicitly ever present meaning cast by the title over this collection. A "country" of impossibility, perhaps, yet one *from which* new departure remains to be, is willed to be, taken. The liminal epigraph, quoting Michaux--"*Dans un réseau de lignes fatales, s'enfonce l'imprudent qui prononça une parole irréfléchie*"--may constitute *a* pole of psychological and creative consciousness; but the title unquestionably provides new polarity and ekes out a poetics of design, desire and determination. Sobering images may thus continue to prevail but a future light shines forth, perhaps that of the closing poem, "Le Jour tient..." (LP, 30), where fires glints once more and an after-time to love's lived storm is glimpsed:

> Des oiseaux font une buée dans l'orage
> Sous le voile du soleil
> ils prennent feu
> Du sel crépite dans leurs ailes
> après l'amour.

Juste avant la nuit appears two years after *Le Pays d'où j'irai*, in 1979. Despite many persistent tensions, its form, like that of *Le Pays d'où j'irai*, moreover, demonstrates a reinvigoration and new creativeness that, like the latter's title, succeed in beaming light across a landscape on the verge of utter blackness. If *Le Pays d'où j'irai* offers ontic renewal via a new poeticity dependent on very compact free verse structures, a total absence of punctuation and a complete erasure of first and second person pronouns, *Juste avant la nuit* textually "accomplishes" in the face of raw non-accomplishment by structuring itself as a "poème en deux tableaux"-- the subtitle thereby hints broadly at the earlier thematics of parallels, doubling, chiasma, separation, dissociation, differenciation--and by further adapting non-rhyming versified form and intertwined roman and italic "voice" to a more fluid, continuous format, where unity seems synonymous with multifacettedness and even duality. The decision made by Anne Teyssiéras to theatricise in *tableaux* seems to allow a more distantiated, somewhat mythical treatment of urgent, visceral imagery. The first texts of each *tableau* are critical here, and there is a constant interplay of voice, a continuous shifting of distance and perspective marked by pronominal usage. The first of these liminal texts privileges closure, wornness, lifelessness. Exit implies return; dusk deepens--we are exactly *Juste avant la nuit*; and, as ever, confrontation and exchange are the order of the barely remaining day. The second liminal text places the "characters" in a barren space, but a space displaying the site of speech. Beyond, lies one of Rimbaud's possibly splendid cities. The linked texts of *tableau I* offer much bleakness, a blackness colouring the soul, linguistic and emotional impotence, a sense of spinning around within mirror reflections and obsessions, but it can, too, show an awareness of feasible resolution: letting the "knot" of being unravel naturally, understanding that the locus of lamentation can be one of triumph, that chiasma is a figure of choice and decision, and not just of fatal interweaving. *Tableau II* stages a recognition of the impossibility of the re-)union of self and other, whilst marking their continued "entanglement of speech". The invocation of and fusion with the voice of the other ties its logic inextricably to the will to free the self from fatality, from that predestined "signature" attached to lives: such is the aporetic, chiasmal structure of Teyssiéras' imagination. *Juste avant la nuit* is a solemn, intense, simple and yet infinitely complex saga. If it recognises the illusion upon which it rides--"J'ai conçu ma demeure sur l'îlot d'une illusion" (JA, 30)--, it perceives too the beauty and depth of a dream no more illusory than life itself:

> Mère sois sauve dans le retrait
> Sois présente dans l'écart
> Sois l'élue de ce lieu que nul n'habite
> encore   (JA, 31).

Three years later, in 1982, Teyssiéras republishes *Parallèles*, but appends to it *Boule de cristal*, her notes for an *ars poetica* that will fully blossom in 1986 with the publication of *Les Clavicules de Minho*. Such self-reflexive work is very much in the modernist French tradition since Baudelaire and Mallarmé and has stubbornly persisted through poets such as Reverdy and Char, Deguy and Bonnefoy, Du Bouchet and Dupin. Teyssiéras sees poetry as absence, an action without a place, a stripping of the self via abandonment to desire. On the other hand, poetry "peoples" desire, its texts constituting an anti-topographical *relief*, "une dentelle d'écume" (BC, 42) upon the endless swell of being. Curiously, moreover, it can be seen as possessing a superiority over its very subject, its actual motivation, touching an infinite strangely linked to "nothingness", knowing ecstasy even in anguish (BC, 43). The divine may be sensed only negatively, as absence, yet even such disenchantment remains "un désenchantement enchanté" (BC, 45). The polarities of desire thus tend to define poetry's psychological (non-)space, yet no stable equations, even oppositional, may be said to be articulated. The self's "immensity" is somehow sensed to be experienceable via poetic blind seeing, though within the "narrowing of the mental field" oddly in correspondence with such vastness and infinity (BC, 47). Thus is it, perhaps, that Anne Teyssiéras can, despite her earlier proclamation, declare that poetic action has "quelque chose à voir avec une Divinité. / Cette divinité me sacre et me défait" (BC, 48): an undoing and remaking of the self in the intuitive, simultaneous experience of sacredness and absence, nothingness, even derision. "To write", she argues, is to risk "fix[ing] vertigoes" such as these, though once more Teyssiéras' poetics lies at an intersection joining factors of resolution, ephemeralness and "foamy" provisionality, and a self-petrification tantamount to immolation, of self, of other.

Poèmes en Kabbale (1984), to which I cannot give attention here, separates these complex tusslings with the logic of the poet's action from those developed in much more ample detail in *Les Clavicules de Minho*. A book of linked yet fragmented and densely compact reflections upon poetic voice and indeed all artistic expression, *Les Clavicules de Minho* is a book to be reckoned with in profundity and authenticity every bit as much as the writings of Bonnefoy, Deguy or Noël. No pretentiousness, no tendentiousness, are manifest. Poetry and art, for Anne Teyssiéras, offer an oddly intransitive knowledge, a kind of "laughter... in response to all questions" (CM, 7). They are predicated upon "belief", desire, "promise"; they hesitate between sense and non-sense; their "focussing" is illusory, their contact is with nothingness; they both delight in and "dismiss" their place of origin and anchorage: earth; they function as *détour*, metaphenomenality as it were, though they offer a "Way"--of relativity, passingness, non-absoluteness. Founded upon an intuition of a merely approximate and convenient structure, the poetic or artistic gesture

112

does not possess specifiable logic and delimitable meaning. Such gesture, and the trace it leaves, are, one might say, living "deconstruction". The poet, as Teyssiéras says, "s'abrite... dans l'oeil du cyclone, tandis que tu t'épuises aux franges du non-sens" (CM, 43). Poetry and art are thus "un déplacement non un aboutissement" (CM, 55). Myth, she rightly argues, comes precisely from poetry's, art's, "detour" or distanciation. Other forces, however, are infinitely greater, and, possibly, less mystifying: love, the forces of being beyond us, the distant "effusion" of which poetry and art are but an "echo" (CM, 88). The latter are merely "la salive du néant" (CM, 101)--but, let us remember, "tout est dans Rien" (CM, 40)-- and require our smiling, compassionate but lucid laughter to show both their skeletalness and their residual potential for illumination. The texts of *Les Clavicules de Minho*, despite their ellipses, density, multiple fragmentations and aporias, seek to provide definition, coherence and clarification. They are even orchestrated, whether *a priori* or *a posteriori* we do not know, into seven "chapters" followed by seven "cadences". Overall--and they do stand as a configuration, one readable backwards as profitably as forwards, and in that sense as fluid, as unfinished or uncongealed, as the poem itself--overall, then, they offer a remarkably sensitive and vastly ranging meditation eked out curiously enough from one of the most concentrated and finely focussed *œuvres* we have dealt with here. Such a vastness, however, reveals that "immensity" of the self of which *La Boule de cristal* spoke, and reminds us that the poetics underpinning the most concise artform gives to the latter an implicit, though often masked infinity. To reread Teyssiéras in the light of *Les Clavicules de Minho* is, at minimum, to inflate her finitude in the direction of this infinity.

113

Le Chemin sous la mer appears in 1992 and one can quickly perceive in it a continuity of tone and emotion taking us all the way back to *Epervier ma solitude* and *Fragments pour une captive* and hovering between the serenity of a Heather Dohollau and the restless questioning of an Edmond Jabès. This continuity gives an immediately compelling and intense validity to a collection riding, further, upon the hidden intricacies, *danses* and *contre-danses* (CM, 74), of *Les Clavicules de Minho*. The collection opts, further, for a discreet intertextual and citational mode that is very consciously structured whilst avoiding all impression of aesthetic or ideational closure. The book, however, is manifestly meditational, struggles as ever with the large questions of life and death, refuses conservative oppositions incarnated in language and tending to "strangulation" or "oblivion" (LC, 13) or the ceaseless churnings of the self without liberation. For Teyssiéras, here, the question, the mosaical perception, seem to offer the most apt anti-locus of poetical and ontological residence: ephemeral, moving, non-absolute, yet teemingly plural, possible. Being, in Teyssiéras' poetics, is thus less definable in terms of visible, achieved constructs than according to that which "calls" and summons us, those voids and possibles continually and temporarily (ful)-filled. And yet this "call" of being remains linked to memory, to origin, to some "*beacon* beyond the world" (LC, 33). Leaving behind the free verse forms adopted in the 1970's, *Le Chemin sous la mer* reverts--apart from its prologue--to a prose at once syntactically continuous and semantically lacunary. *Points de suspension* and certain textual or typographical rhythmic effects further complicate the lacunae of meaning, and the *index de la symbolique des lettres* (of the ten chapter titles, from "Lamed" to "Shin") demonstrates the further layering this meaning constantly undergoes. The whole, moreover, lies under the (additional)

114

sign of Marina Tsvetaeva: "Se laisser anéantir jusqu'au tout dernier atome, qui de résister (et d'en réchapper) fait naître le monde". The prologue in itself (LC, 9) is, despite its residual simplicity, so dense, so tranquilly seething with (dis)continuous, polysemic metaphor, that a whole essay could barely do it justice. Its poetics hinges on conceivable resolution or synthesis of extremes, of differences; on the tensions of *faille*, rupture, marredness or perhaps merely *pliure*, and knowledge, knowableness; on questions of use and disuse; on factors of cyclicalness and passingness; on laughter as simple unfoldment and laughter as characteristic telluric violence; on ontic and poetic oozing or frothing as "angelic" events questioning our most basic sociological and psychological assumptions, or as events quite beyond "innocence", marred, tortured mysteries. Each of the chapters following, which, however, constitute a typically complex mosaic wherein one element does not dominate others-- each chapter explores manifest or implicit aspects of the prologue, aspects often allegorically elaborated, but which Teyssiéras conceptually telescopes in her index (LC, 77). The final chapter, "Shin" (LC,71-4), should not then be read as a climax to some linear logic, it too is movement, "displacement[,] not accomplishment". Madness and errancy are possible forms of being, no doubt ever within us all, ever part of the tensions of the absurd and the sacred, the fleeting and the absent, the trace and the all/nothingness of experience--bizarre jewels in the invisible crown of our enigma.

ESTHER TELLERMANN

It is only in 1986 that Esther Tellermann's first collection, *Première apparition avec épaisseur*, appears, with Flammarion's series, "Textes". Offered as a "journal métaphysique", it seeks to articulate those points of intersection of the "quotidian" and the "imperceptible", where surface attains to some depth and phenomena attach themselves to at least tentative meaning. The "autobiography" that ensues establishes distance both voluntarily via the discretion of its veiled scenes, personas and events, and involuntarily through the lived difficulties of utterance; but its mission remains clear: a "recherche du sens" that, without ever acceding to the "subjectivité brûlante" surprisingly evoked, nevertheless etches out a direction and an articulation quite distinctive. The book's title, of course, hints at literary, incarnational and meditative beginnings, whilst conjuring up both some Pongian *épaisseur*--of things *and* words--and the aporetic vision of the opaqueness of either. The *table des matières*, not blatantly presented as such and offered at the opening of the book, has the effect of obliging us to read through the essential symbols of Tellermann's *univers imaginaire* as if, almost, it were a poem in its own right: a poem of erasure, of masked essential purpose; of nevertheless absolute phenomenal being; of reversal of optic, of non-measurement, of vibration, rhythm, pulsion; of questions of image, choice, "writing one's order"; of death; of re-viewing "le même objet", and so on.

As we move into the collection, what strikes us initially is less the firmness and coherence of some developing discourse or described action or set of emotions, but rather the difficulty experienced in settling meaning into place, inclining the metaphors and designations towards some continuity, establishing even the pertinence of details focussed upon.

116

And yet a great simplicity and, in a sense, clarity remain within isolated lines. From stanza to stanza and even from line to line, however, a poetics of discontinuity and unanchorableness often persists, bringing density and enigma to the simple, a semantic unrootableness to the referentially rootable. Mildly characteristic of such tensions is the text ending the first section of "LA CHAMBRE MASQUE L'OBJET", "efface", where, if we feel we have a firm initial grasp of things, not only does semantic-referential slippage set in, but it is a somewhat precarious venture to relate the stanzas to the two titles hovering over them:

> Transit
> sur une terre durcie.
> Rien n'estompe le cru.
> L'humide n'est que
> halètement.
> Pourquoi s'agripper au feu quand le noir se retourne.
>
> Il suffit
> que le blanc s'efface
> vous êtes
> l'ondulation du vent.   (PA, 16)

Such abrupt, punctuated or unpunctuated adjacencies arguably mime the infinitely fragmented and joined mosaicalness of being, of experience. Tellermann's theatricalisation of the components of her experience of being comes about, as much great theatre does, with a minimum or total absence of contextualisation. The risk of such utterance is that it become esoteric, self-absorbed, but we can see from the above text that, despite our uncertainties--where are we? why? what is the connection between dampness and *halètement*? what fire and what blackness? and what whiteness? etc.--, we understand that this poem provides a series of flickering images that are far from Mallarméan, nor even Rimbaldian in mode: travel through perhaps barren country, sharp contours, light and insufficient dew?, a sensitivity to brightness and darkness, their movement, their emotional weight, the caress of the wind upon the face. From a minimalness, perhaps much uncertainty as to the deep significance of life's components, and even a natural element of literary *pudeur*, emerges throughout *Première apparition avec épaisseur* a high implicitness, a laconic richness that form and structure serve to encourage.

The collection stresses repeatedly notions of "walking/Learning" (PA, 27); of a *parcours* at once concrete and spiritual (PA, 28); of a traversal of "présence" Tellermann never ceases discreetly to meditate: "des masses d'air séparaient la parole" (PA, 20); of a need sensing the unseen, the "goldenness" of greyness, for example, or "des regards au-delà / perdus" (PA, 29). The shifting "why" of existence hovers everywhere, in the questions posed and the enigmas articulated; hope now may be thought fragile, now seemingly recuperated: "Mais j'ai dit les bleus infinis / quand le regard adoucit la lumière" (PA, 30). Tellermann's poetry resists blatancy, however, preferring to record the fleeting glimmerings of otherness in the ephemeral everywhere: "Tout peut être image / chaque ailleurs dans chaque passage" (PA, 34). This, as she realises, involves a "tending towards the obscure", a pushing far of some inner gaze (PA, 39) and a sense of the self's improbable "control" of being, despite puzzlement, recurrent fears and feelings of *affadissement* and *ressassement* (PA, 44): "Qui te balance au flux de l'éclatement solaire / Sinon toi?" (PA, 40).

The opening of part 5, "vibrer l'air" (PA, 49), appears particularly valuable for an understanding of Tellermann's early poetics:

Parmi les signes
ne nie pas.
Casse la rigueur.
Le sacré encore te dresse.

118

A telegraphic self-prescription is thus quickly mapped out: existentially and poetically, embrace of and assent to the earth's "signs" need to be as it were undiscriminating; a culling out and refusal of certain signs is undesirable, for inadequately open, aware; the "rigour" of system, intellectualisation--i.e. selection and reduction--is to be broken; the "sacredness" of life's totality is a preferred guide. This does not mean that dispersal, distance and excessiveness cannot be experienced, negatively, as the liminal text of "il écrit son ordre", "'Il avait été chassé de la simplicité de son origine'..." (PA, 70), suggests. Oblivion can set in, as the same sequence insists, yet the poet's task is one of waiting, patience, gathering and inscription of being's music, "cracked" though it may be (PA, 70-71)--such an ontic music, or vibration, being at once of the earth, but, inevitably, of the self:

Je veux te dire qui je suis   (PA, 72).

That such a telling of the self's identity is caught between factors of what Tellermann calls "exactitude dans le sol", expressive "vacillation" and "éclosion de l'enfoui"--concrete blatancy, problems of language and revelations from the unconscious or the intuited--, many texts make clear (PA, 86). And it is equally clear that *Première apparition avec épaisseur* regards all phenomena, gestures, fragments of thought and emotion as palimpsests of each other and of what is at once her "story" and "History" (PA, 101), ever ordered/disordered by "[un] regard interne / qui toujours le[s] portera" (PA, 103). Poetry as a form of retention, as an "historicising" gesture against time, as "l'Histoire [qui] est dans vos boucles" (PA, 108), as a mere but crucial "appearance / with density" (PA, 111).

Trois plans inhumains appears three years later, in 1989, and whilst its overall modal quality may be said to be very similar to that of

119

Première apparition avec épaisseur--enigmaticalness and simplicity fused, semantic and referential looseness, compaction and ellipsis, repetition, concentration and yet wide availability--its structuration is significantly modified. Whereas the 1986 collection opts commonly for more fluid and longer free-verse forms and a manifest exploitation of white space, *Trois plans inhumains* tightens poetic structure so consistently that, of the 124 poems composing the five parts of the volume, 18 are of 2 lines, 33 of 3, 42 of 4, 11 of 5, 11 of 6, 4 of 7, and 5 of 8 lines. Such tightening is reflected in the stanzaic division of the poems, 56 being single structures, 60 divided simply into two short stanzaic blocks, and only 8 divided into three stanzas. Line-length is equally tightened, emphasised by abundant use of the fullstop, and *points de suspension*, whilst on the one hand opening up structure, close down its firm semantic function and emphasise the laconicalness and unsayableness of Tellermann's discourse. The latter, the poet explains, still may be read as a "journal poétique", plunged into factors of "exil, origine et retour [qui] travaillent une quête où le risque affleure à se confondre au mythe de son nom: Quête de l'Idéal, du Double, de la Verticalité dans les monuments et les ruines" (back cover). Esther Tellermann also stresses for the first time an element of derisiveness that can attach to the emerging poem she offers, perhaps because of the latter's perceived "répétition" (repetitiousness and theatrical self-rehearsal) "applied to the world" (*ibid.*). Yet, as with *Première apparition avec épaisseur*, her poetry, as *jeu*, is less sheer play, than interplay of rhythmic components, "chaque variation l'arrachant et la rapportant à la grammaire de son identité" (*ibid.*).

The tenth text of the first suite reads as follows:

> Achètent des boules de sel.
> D'autres sons
> mais le corps se plie.   (TP, 20)

The eleventh and final text of the same suite I shall quote, too, in order to provide a fuller flavour of the volume's opening mode and preoccupations:

> Nous avons interrompu l'histoire.
> C'était pour la ligne tracée
> ce mouvement perpétuel qui ne s'écartait pas.
>
> (TP, 21)

Knowing that the collection is centred upon a journey along the River Nile, we can confirm at once the exoticism and the simplicity of the actions thus very vaguely contextualised. Observation and non-designation nevertheless vie constantly for ascendency: who is buying? what sounds? what body? why focus on a body bending? events and moments are thus isolated, rendered with a certain clarity, yet all explicitness is pushed to one side: Tellermann opts, impulsively, compulsively, for the strangeness, the incoherence of the simple, intact, but unveiled by logical grill. The second poem given above follows this modal pattern. At one level all seems transparent, utterly perceptible: at another we are at a complete loss to answer many questions that inevitably arise: who are "we"? what story has been interrupted? what was "pour la ligne tracée"?: the "perpetual movement not moving away"? and, if so, what does this refer to? Statements dominate the poem, then, but lectoral questions abound and remain. And yet, taking the two poems together, and in the context of all that precedes, an atmosphere still prevails, over and above enigmaticalness, of mythical, eternal gestures, presences, elements of being. Thus is it that the collection as a whole leaves us with a clear

121

impression of having traversed something essential to existence: charming elements such as "le roux [qui] se découvrait / nous remontions la saison" (TP, 35); efforts to understand the meaning of "une main posée. / Le rouge de l'accomplissement" (TP, 31); the sensation of "[la] pluie [qui] apaise un peu de sang" (TP, 43); the author's endeavour to "guette[r] / l'origine déplacée" of things, here (TP, 94); but experiences, too, of loss, "Man['s] dissonance or vibration" (TP, 39), the difficulty in confronting night and "appeasing" death (TP, 69), and so on--the thematics (but the word conveys inadequately the poetic intentions of Tellermann) of *Trois plans inhumains* is near-infinite, for centred in every fragment, fragmented into endless centres of attention.

"Je veux construire..." (TP, 36) is a short text that speaks of construction and a consequent choice of the "arbitrary", and in some measure it would appear to evoke this combined poetics of the infinitesimal and the central, the partial and the pertinent. Tellermann's poetics, however, I should argue, seeks and strains, rather than simply noting passively: if an "arbitrariness" is involved, it is certainly "chosen", assumed, probed; an effort continues to "associe[r] colline et syntaxe", as she writes (TP, 38). An acceptance of the enigmatic must occur (TP, 41), but this does not bring the poetic quest to an abrupt end. Tellermann neither works "form", wishing rather to "escape" from it (TP, 53), nor seeks to avoid the various "suspensions" that her writing inevitably produces (TP, 52). The incompletion of her inscriptions matches a poetics of non-reproduction (TP, 59) in a textual atmosphere where joining and discontinuity curiously combine their logics. Things seen, like the (dis)connecting words that record their passage, are thus savoured precisely because they are enigmatical, half-real, half-dreamed, "historical" and ephemeral at the same time:

Caressent la forme emportée
Parce qu'elle ne sera.   (TP, 115)

To modify the teeming phenomena of the world via an overly tampering mediation is thus not Tellermann's poetic purpose: "'Là devrait être' / a blessé le signe quotidien", she writes (TP, 116). Her breaking, fragmenting mode may perhaps be even seen as a conscious effort to "break off" from a too perfect, too smoothly articulated expression of (her) being, and an invitation to the reader not to glue and seal the poem's lacunae but to bear them up with her:

Comprenez
sa façon de s'arrêter.

Et si le son se brise
le porterez-vous?   (TP, 152)

The question of the "accountability" of our signs which Esther Tellermann poses (TP, 153) is moreover a most modern one: Barthes and Derrida, Bonnefoy and Du Bouchet, and, of course, in a different light, Groult, Irigaray, Hyvrard and Cixous, have shown us the range of complexity of our semiosis. It is sufficient, however, that the poetic taking account of being we witness in *Trois plans inhumains* simply "come across", broken, breaking, beyond strict measurement, for "l'onde / n'est pas mesurable", as Tellermann declares in closing (TP, 158):

Ce lieu peigné
parvint.
De façon fragmentaire.   (TP, 156)

Her hope and belief, manifestly, is that "History will have retained / the unaccomplished gesture" (TP, 149), and, perhaps less manifestly, that her poetic dreaming, "doubling" angles and levels of approach will accede to a sense of our otherness, our ideality, our depth, whilst triumphing over fears, cruelty and hellishness.

123

Esther Tellermann's most recent collection, *Distance de fuite* (1993), offers what Claude Esteban has termed "quelques notations furtives" founded upon a sense of aporia, absence and impasse despite the blatant presence and abundance of the "impeccable geometry of the world" (back cover). Unrhymed free verse continues, with highly compact lines, but the really short poetic structures fade noticeably (1 x 2 lines, 8 x 3 lines), whereas, of the 79 poems, the tight middle lengths continue to dominate: 24 x 4 lines, 15 x 5 lines, 18 x 6 lines, with the other structures as follows: 6 x 7 lines, 6 x 8 and one of 9 lines. Much formal continuity thus reigns from *Trois plans inhumains* to *Distance de fuite*. Whilst we might therefore feel that Tellermann has found and confirmed her poetic form and, indeed, mode--for ellipsis, non-contextualisation, unfocussed but richly allusive referentiality, a semantic quality ranging from the crisply transparent yet open to the obscure, even the hermetic, and so on, persist unabated--, we should not forget that an overall poetics of existential difficulty and dogged quest manifest itself in *Distance de fuite* and that this may well lead to radical modal and formal transformations in due course. Imaginatively or thematically, the fascination of presence and its relation to time and "History" continue, as the opening text so subtly, so discreetly, yet so powerfully, shows:

> Le détail du gypse
> à partir des cendres
> issues du corps foudroyé.

> Pliait-il l'Histoire?   (DF, 13)

The earth's multitudinous phenomena seem so absolute, so "exact" (DF, 76, 87), and yet so questionable, so open to both emotional doubt and metaphysical inquiry, reexamination. What becomes more evident in *Distance de fuite*, however, is the extent to which writing is an activity--

temporarily? permanently?--"pour contourner la douleur" (DF, 23). What Tellermann calls "le tragique du cadre" (DF, 25)--a framework at once, one senses, highly personal and externalised, theatricalised as in *Trois plans inhumains*--assumes a more major, though still distanced, significance; whilst the simple things of the world are looked to, as the epigraph to *Distance de fuite* suggests, to "lull her paleness" (DF, 24):

> "Je t'apprendrai à regarder les pierres
> les scarabées aveugles
>
> les fragments en taille de poussière d'étoiles."
>
> (DF, 7)

Récit or poetic text can thus seem even synonymous with exile at certain moments (DF, 49), though Tellermann shows sensitivity to the idea that outer states reflect our inner states, that matter is always "la matière du vertige" (DF, 47), a projection, a real-isation of an interior gestalt. Thus is it, I should argue, that Tellermann sees, feels, can still create, "dans la tradition du désespoir", as she ironically writes, the possible beauty, one much more difficult to see, feel and create, because beyond irony, of "un feu virtuel" (DF, 14). "De quoi peupler le cri? / L'enjeu", she pointedly writes (DF, 16); upon reflection, and conditionally, tentatively, she answers, like a René Char, or a Chantal Chawaf or a Janine Mitaud:

> Nous recommencerions
> à partir du vert.   (DF, 16)

To dwell in melancholia and its poetic, romantico-symbolist equivalents-- from *l'élégie* to *la complainte* or even *le tombeau*--does not sit well with Esther Tellermann. "'Transforme la plainte / en polyphonie'", she commands; silence is to be adorned / parried (DF, 73, 89), and this may involve, as the simple, moving "Les eaux vertes ont perdu ma soeur..." (DF, 74) suggests, shifting poetic tactics further between what she calls "caméra et cri", lucidity and sheer emotion, recording and expressionism.

Certainly, in a different perspective, the choice between "le fruit et l'otage" (DF, 47), fructification and imprisonment, though perhaps difficult to effect, is clear to make for Tellermann. *Distance de fuite* is the "history" of a tacit accomplishment that, traversing the lacerations of waiting and the fluctuations of "prayer", may only result in "putting off pain", but this is never any mean accomplishment:

Attente comme tessons.

-Je n'avais pour prier que le balancement.
Elle a reporté sa douleur.   (DF, 68)

Such deferral allows, precisely, for a "skimming of worlds / of shimmerings" (DF, 91), for a deft, dutiful grasping of what flits by at a point where things would otherwise slip away: "Vous deviez saisir le galop / à la distance de fuite" (DF, 101).

"Sur la cassure..." (DF, 100) is one of the closing poems of *Distance de fuite*:

Sur la cassure du monde
le regard n'embrassait pas
ni le mot ne réduisait la plaine
les chaos nous menaient
vers les lieux contenus.

It speaks, of course, not only of telluric, planetary crisis--who knows? ecological, physical, socio-political, but undoubtedly spiritual, in the broadest sense of the term--, but also of poetico-linguistic impotence and general human unlovingness, indifference, unwillingness. The atmosphere of chaos and limited spaciousness only confirms the initial elements of Tellermann's *imaginaire* and, needless to say, contrasts radically with the poetics of resistance and resilience the collection achieves. An earlier poem--reading the volume backwards--, "Villa peinte..." (Df, 78) is quite

126

differently instructive, however, and corrects what will have to serve as our conclusion:

> Ville peinte.
> Les plans hauts des jardins
> interrompent la falaise
> un Ange écrit la scène
> des trois paysages
> par identification à l'air.

Here we are back in a poem observing the simple fullness of the earth, the eye straying beyond self-consciousness over town, terraced gardens, cliff, absorbing presence's unspeakable absoluteness, the mind and the heart, however, finally attributing a surprising origin to the beauty of the seen: some "angelic" hand of discreet creative power: air, light, the unsung mediums of the seeable. The poem thus rises high above pain, moves away from the self, sensing yet the pertinence for all in her one sudden intuition. What is at stake, a still earlier poem had asked, if not knowing how to "people one's cry" (DF, 16)? Esther Tellermann instinctively, though conditionally, replied on a note of spring-like resilience:

> Nous recommencerions
> à partir du vert.   (DF, 16)

MARIE-CLAIRE BANCQUART

Since the publication in 1972 of the slim but elegant and tensely urgent *Projets alternés*, Marie-Claire Bancquart's work has blossomed in various, undoubtedly complementary ways. Although principally given to poetry, and professionally involved in this domain also, she has written five novels down to the recent *Photos de famille* (1989) and *La Saveur du sel* (1993), and edited or offered critical assessments of, beyond the field of contemporary poetry, the work of Maupassant, *fin de siècle* Paris, the Nobel prize-winning Anatole France, and surrealism, and, most recently, the full span of the twentieth century. *Projets alternés* may, upon initial reflection, seem somewhat remote from such developments, but it already pertinently establishes what she deems, and will continue to deem, the dualistic, divided state of both the world at large and her own innermost sense of being-in-the-world. The opening poem, taking up the volume's title, suggests that dualism is not mere fatalism, but involves choice, option, an action tussling with love and clinical knowledge, peace and perversion, happiness and annihilation. Whilst, then, a poetics may quickly develop of loss of dream and supple vitality, of failure and suicide, of lassitude, ruin and imminent apocalypse--a poetics wherein poetry itself is reduced to mere "rature sur balafre" (PA, 14)--Bancquart remains sensitive to our residual capacity for "deconstruct[ing] the world" (PA, 16) via a power of love that risks oblivion. To hope to accomplish even some minimal reversal of a reigning bleakness and disquietude, Bancquart appreciates already the significance of time, all time, now: "Vivre dans la seconde entre bourgeon et feuille", in the dynamism, the surging possibility of that tight but exquisite space of ontic fullness, the only one, ever-now, available to us. "Retour" (PA, 17) evokes this feasibility, as does "Repénétré" (PA, 21-22), where renascence, psychic and telluric reinvigoration rules the imagination. "Le corps incomparable de l'amour / Le corps refusé de l'amour" (PA 24): here seems the true intersection of our being, practicable, exposed to our desire, our will, utterly choosable. Such a choice appears, moreover, more straightforward than our resolution of the question of the divine--Bancquart speaks of "la Face problématique" that could lead to upstaging Pascal in "gambling God double or quits" (PA, 26)--but we might see "love" and "divineness" as equivalent contemporary metaphors. *Projets alternés* confronts lyrical blockage--the collection's final two poems, "Lyre morte" and "Mots et guerre" (PA, 28-9) are singularly eloquent here--but comes to understand well the broad struggle lying ahead, the ironically precarious status of all expression of even residual transcendence today. "Dans ta caresse / Gauche abondance de fruits" (PA,28).

Mains dissoutes appears in 1975 and offers a compactly compelling extension of initial preoccupations. Its overall tendency, however, veers somewhat more visibly not only towards factors of resistance and recuperation--resistance to "la grande pétrification de la démence" (MD, 10), recuperation of "un monde ressaisi dans l'extrémité morte de l'exil" (MD, 23)--but towards a further clarification of the feasible elements of recuperation. Thus, in order to spin, from the raw, bloodied fleece of existence, "une étoffe à recouvrir la ténacité de sa tristesse" (MD, 4), can Bancquart point to the deep psychological, ethical and spiritual purpose of an attention given to what Bonnefoy terms "the things of the simple". "Par un oiseau nous accédons à l'éloge soulevé / Par l'ombre à la présence sans défaut" (MD, 22), we read; and such birds and shadows step out of metaphoricity, rhetoric, all suggestion of inward-turning poetic conceit: they are experienced presence, a path of nomination leading back to the earth's splendour and mystery. "Et c'est l'abeille qui comprend", Bancquart pointedly affirms, "au mépris des / cueilleurs de phrases" (MD, 8). "To comb the dawn and forget all hateful, dirty sleep" (MD, 8) is neither an invitation to dispense with dream, nor an encouragement to return to idle romanticism; rather is it a simple urging upon us of the possible caress of the natural mystery forever with us, and an accompanying reminder to awaken from the morass of paralysing oblivion rendering us unconscious of such feasibility. The volume's opening text, "Ville" (MD, 1), thus evokes the "coagulation"--and hence, possible decoagulation--of a natural human "angelicism": not that of some horror-stricken *symboliste*, but that based upon our inner propensity for love, poised as we are upon "les vasques du songe", though slipping towards "des rives problématiques". "A l'opposé" (MD, 16) not dissimilarly speaks of hope and the promise of the simple--"l'herbe / le boeuf la laine accrochés aux clôtures"--, whilst stressing the latter's vulnerability and delicacy, caught as they are between "un éclat futur" and "un soleil promis à pourriture". The closing text, "Incidence de lune" (MD, 28-9), whilst not ceasing to dwell within a consciousness of resentment, violence and "suppuration", recalls to us the innocence of the earth's quiet continuity and "inner face"; factors of belonging and interconnection; "la transparence du bonheur" available to lovers. If, then, "l'incidence de lune est exode et naissance", exodus can be seen not just as flight before the disturbances of the world, but as a rhythmic, repossibilising flow, providing renewal through refusal, rebirth through death.

The 1978 *Mémoire d'abolie* constitutes a substantial collection of poems, articulated in four parts: "Marges", "D'une fougère bleue les veines", "La Peau les os", "Arcane sans couronne". These sectional titles already hint broadly at the sharper focus to come: motifs of marginalisation, discretion and inconspicuousness; the lure of the subtle tracery of the things of the earth; consciousness of body, its mortal fragility, yet its multiple and lasting lessons for us and others; the enigma of existence, at once glorious and disturbing, and beyond older notions of regality or heavenly aura, and so on. Marie-Claire Bancquart has, moreover, a clear, if necessarily elliptical poetic project in mind with *Mémoire d'abolie*. "Écrire: pour le désordre du monde", she states,

> pour les routes disséminées de notre espace intérieur. Mais, aussi, écrire pour le lieu ramassé du corps à corps.
> Lieu passager, lieu des limites, le poème est dans l'ellipse.
> Faire-part des difficultés, il habite aussi des mots inhabitables: l'arbre, le sang, l'amour.
> Écrire: pour posséder sa mort.   (MA, cover)

Such a programme is, primarily, a project *for* what is, a project at once ethical, social, spiritual, telluric. All "paths", interior and external, are relevant to this programme, being mutually pertinent, reciprocally symbolic. Poetic language finds itself in the paradoxical position of pointing, falteringly, to what it is not, to what it cannot represent, being merely--but crucially--sign: the logic of externality (: "treeness"), the logic even of the self's physicality (: "blood"), the logic of, not merely thought, but exquisite emotion ("love"). And all of this in order to occasion a possession, here and now, of one's mortal, ephemeral possibility.

Throughout this major collection, Bancquart will emphasise the complexities of the use of language, its convolutions, its being caught in the crossfire of multiple discourses, the fact that, whilst desiring definition, joy, immediate being, and whilst relishing much of its metaphorical and endlessly interpersonal interplay, language can be constantly confused and fouled up with bitterness (MA, 19). Such bitterness--planetary, not at all essentially personal-- stems undoubtedly, in its turn, from the sentiments of rejection, "unliving", self-explosion, drift and non-alignment that people Bancquart's *univers imaginaire* and that render all intercourse between any *je* and any *tu* precarious, partial, incoherent. "Ce que je suis le presque rien / Le déconstruit / de moi / vers toi" (MA, 57). Such felt "deconstruction" of imaginable networks of communion does not block poetic (: creative, regenerative) desire, however. *Mémoire d'abolie* teems with desire, simple, yet multifarious desire. "J'habite", explains Bancquart in one of many pertinent poems, "un grand désir de déhiscence" (MA, 54): a need, psychological and visceral, to open the self, like an iris or a fern, to its infinite contents and the mysterious fullness without. The "simplest warmth" can thus be sought or a caressed, awaited silence (MA, 40), desire unfolding upon "le positif de moi grâce aux ténèbres d'à-côté" (MA, 48). Or, at other moments, as "Mémoire d'abolie" powerfully reveals, desire may risk that self-explosion earlier feared, seeing in it not a disappearance, but rather an action so authentic as to achieve some quasi-Rimbaldian self-recovery elsewhere, *other-wise*:

> Rêve:
> se flibuster
> se canonner
> se couler à la fin, trop heureux d'être absentée des rôles
> par une opération personnelle.   (MA, 99)

Considering such modes of (self-)achievement, it is perhaps not surprising to see Bancquart espouse a minimalism, a *poétique du peu*, that has much, though varyingly, prospered from Mallarmé and Jarry to Michaux and Beckett, Ponge and Duras, a consciousness of spatial, temporal and ontological minimality that yet deems it too easy to "enter negation", resisting the latter, choosing desire, even wild dream, in order to "prophesy passage" (MA, 117), to catch even the most ephemeral of loves: "ta mort dans la main / Tu aimes le monde / Une minute" (MA, 135). Such veering, through minimalness, residualness, away from negation towards self's / all selves' positiveness, requires an "improvisation" (MA, 162) and an "intuition" (MA, 165) leading not surprisingly to the ellipses we have seen Bancquart hold inevitable, poetically. Such forces are real, however, profoundly active, and need not worry us; they are part of our true apprehension of being's gentleness. "C'est doucement le jour si tu ne l'effraies pas" (MA, 176).

Another major collection appears in 1981: *Partition*. One year earlier a small number of poems of the volume had been published separately under the title, *Voix* (1980), with eight *reliefs* by Marc Pessin. These texts, now incorporated into the first section of *Partition*, "Amour, terrible champ", generate an initial thematics of erosion and haemorrhage, and articulate a chilling "no" to the all too readily exposed myths of "l'homme radieux / la dignité l'amour" (P, 19). Such a "negation", however, is quickly placed in the perspective of a required reclaiming of "un monde habitable" (P, 20), an old, clinging desire for restoration and reinvigoration. If, then, it is essential not to mistake the *plaquette*'s emblematically fragile equilibrium--"j'écris ces lignes entre la mort et moi", Bancquart writes--we are asked equally to remember the "fallow" spaces of being, nearly forgotten, ever available, the fact that "nous débordons la partition" (P, 22): our being is ever, infinitely, in excess of our written score, our account of existence.

Partition swallows up the few texts of *Voix* but their ultimate message rings through its seven substantial sections. All "scores" realisable will not contain the music of being: what is needed is a giving of the self to enigma, to the desire for endless "density" that earth and self experience. "Hongres de Dieu", Bancquart declares us, but "nous tentons

133

nouveaux rêves" (P, 24). Such newly, anti-dogmatically focussed dream may attach itself to "le sacre bleu des pluies sur le cyprès" (P, 12), for, as she argues in "Quand ce serait la fin des minutes", "*the altar may be / a stone bench / an old tree*" (P, 137); but it is true to say, too, that, complementing this "ovation timide vers le monde" (P, 105), there is a marked consciousness of some either actual or feasible all-inclusive *au-delà* (P, 97)--part of the great "unthinkable desire" that can drive on mind and heart, but by no means implying an absolute separation of the immanent and the transcendent, and rather circling back to the sense of enigma to which we might give faith. Poetry, in this context, seems to be an endeavour to bootstrap dreamed "space" into reality: "Je te parle / dans une île que je décris / pour essayer qu'elle soit" (P, 27); its "unique chance" is ever "maintenant / ici / avec" (P, 38)--a "beyond", then, that re-discovers in our given place of being the otherness of the given, stripping away exile (cf. P, 90) through the paradoxical ephemeralness and relativity of words. Poetry, Marie-Claire Bancquart's certainly, may thus operate a kind of consent, it may represent an act of love and endless desire, but it can, as part of this action, "apostrophise the cosmos", question and criticise as intensely as a Lamartine, a Hugo or a Bonnefoy. "*Marcher / pour hommage*", as she puts it (P, 138), is a continuous, shifting process, its celebration is constantly moving with desire and mentation themselves (cf. P, 90) and is, furthermore, caught between its own mortality and its uncompleted vision. Poetry as *mouvance* is thus to "walk / towards definitive transhumance" (P, Tarot XXII), but its accomplishment, being process, ever queries and in a sense defers such definitiveness. "On est l'hôte ambigu", Bancquart affirms towards the end of "Routes" (P, 49-53), "détenteur de lézardes. Enseignes d'insécurité. Telles enseignes. Contre telles assignations du simple". Thus, again, does a poetics of the minimum, the unpretentious and the positively deconstructive raise its voice in *Partition*--in, say, "Pour un spectateur ignoré" (P, 81-4)--but, as Bancquart gently emphasises,

> *mais de ce peu*
> *semence*
> *à tous les verts complémentaires de nos veines*
> *menthe*
> *vitrail*
> *salve des vagues.*

To walk, to pass through, to go forth (: *phalène*) into the enigma of the world's being, is thus, as "*L'Ange arpenteur...*" (P, 119-20) suggests, to merge the logics of the visible and the invisible, to "designate"--via unaccomplishable, unfinishable poetic nomination--"the country one cannot see". It gives credence both to sensual, immediate, experience and to what further buoys up such experience: something we "dig at", "dream of", see emotionally, psychologically. "S'il n'y avait rien, l'espace nous suffirait", Bancquart writes. All "walking" or traversal, and the "homage"--or anguish-- it may produce, are much more than material, physiological, chemical.

The 1983 collection, *Votre visage jusqu'à l'os*, presents four sections with distinct but interlocking emphases. Its overall tone is altogether more bleak, its ambition remaining perhaps that of antiphonal counterpoise to the earlier poetics of celebration and recuperation, delicate as this already is. The gaze it casts upon the face of being thus penetrates to the "bone", to some harder--more difficult, more brutal--articulation. "Je donne en communication journal du noir" (VV, 58), Bancquart explains in the section entitled "Toi", and the poems of the second section are grouped under the title "Autoportraits au noir". A sense of barrenness may thus prevail, cynicism and despondency may press their relevancy,

135

crackedness and derision may seem inevitable. Life "drift[s] upon absence" and language is reduced to the aporetic function of "speaking / so as to be silent aloud" (VV, 50). But, if then the central poetic persona can obsessively declare, "d'une langue dévastée / je lèche passagère habitation du noir" (VV, 57), we read here the telling passingness of such dark existential and psychological dwelling: just as the poetics of walking and traversal represent becoming, transformation, so do they imply moving in, and out of, such blackness. Thus, if "tout amour vire en hivernage" (VV, 58), if "l'univers défaille en nous, palpe une demi-tombe" (VV, 59), so can reversal function in an "opposite", cyclical or rhythmic mode, hibernation almost promising awakening, half-tombality being equally a state of "semi-god[liness]", knotted up with mortality and "buried within the obscure" (VV, 59). The collection's closing section, "Félicités énigmatiques", conveys similar precarious and tense articulations in which "le plein, le vide / s'échangent autour d'une main" (VV, 85) and where resolution cannot escape dialectics, yet cannot attain to happy synthesis. If the correspondence between language and cosmos is "prodigal / of the enigmatic", confidence in the "secrecy" of "our hand"'s creations is rather less manifest. Refusal has for so long been our response to being's mystery that "la maturité des fruits... comme une parole ancienne", as Bancquart writes in the volume's final poem (VV, 92), still risks passing us by, patiently available, undreamed, unmeditated as a unified and unifying locus of meaning.

Recognised in 1984 and 1985 by the attribution of major national literary prizes, Marie-Claire Bancquart's work reaches an exquisite provisional peak of accomplishment with the publication, in 1986, of *Opportunité des oiseaux*. Here, exile is more blatantly matched by a consciousness of intimacy, the "unsinging" that has tempted poets such as

Noël and Roche in different ways blends into the surging "celebrations" Bancquart voices, separation yields more dramatically to a poetics of "inclusion" and "alliance". If a minimalness remains at the base of all creation--"presque rien / est notre garant" (OO, 15)--this does not fundamentally inhibit the latter: risk "the fine risk of [a] sacredness" nothing to do with "God" (OO, 17, 31), gives back to things what they need from us (OO, 19), an opportunity that their own ephemeral opportuneness mirrors and exteriorises--for our recognition. "L'insaisissable est proche", Bancquart therefore comes to understand, beyond the questionable power and "utilité des gnoses" (OO, 25): what consciousness is dealing with is the paradox of the figures of *l'infigurable*, the finite evidence of the infinite. Our inner dis-figurations of being are mimed perhaps by the mysterious disymetries of the maimed, "Enigme" (OO, 39) suggests, and, as a later text states, in the logic of our meta/physical stances, "la dérision n'est pas certaine" (OO, 64).

Marie-Claire Bancquart tells us, with solemnity and smile, that she dreams of some vast, regularly updated poem of existence, an all-embracing, redemptive gesture:

> *Chaque fascicule paraît en lune décroissante, quand il ne*
> *faut couper ni les cheveux, ni les branches des arbres, et*
> *que l'on a besoin de se rappeler le bonheur.*

(OO, 81)

As, for Mallarmé, *Un coup de dés, Opportunité des oiseaux* is one of these "instalments", one of the parts of the dreamed Book or *Grand Oeuvre* in which may be explored, reviewed and sung "[l]'énigme de la fête constante / dans l'usure constante", as Bancquart writes in "Secret" (OO, 94). Such a recuperative embrace of the so easily eroded means that poetry can hope, like plants, to keep our consciousness of presence always critically above the obsessive temptations of absence (cf. OO, 96). The "capital things" of which "we speak little"--"une douceur d'iris et de bestiaux / [qui] jaillit tellement artésienne" (OO, 13), for example--may thus be recognised in their simple fullness. Thanks and gratitude may thus be expressed for the infinitely coloured improbabilities lighting our being, "pour le velu / pour le taché // ... / pour le fauve et l'agile // ... / pour le rejet poussé de nos racines // Pour les cayeux multipliant les bulbes de nos têtes" (OO, 118, "Grâces"). This and other closing poems of the final section, "Alliance", evoke, in a kind of *magnificat* somewhat à la Guillevic but most distinctive, the dark, metamorphic workings of some utterly nameless divinity, traversing you and me, carrots and leeks, reborn outside, but "at the foot" of, some ancient place of worship "setting up its trestles / on the fête" (OO, 119). "De sable", one of these poems, beautifully conjures up these more buoyantly affirmed perceptions, whilst remaining sensitive to the pathetic turmoil of existence:

Crépis les murs avec un long poème d'olives blanches
et consume l'absence
en aimant sexe et peau
tout l'éphémère qui gonfle et te gonfle
à l'image de rues dilatées par un sacre royal.

Oublie l'ombre.

Il y a cette douceur en nous
que rien ne justifie dans l'immense caillot du monde

douceur de gens beaucoup piétinés
qui se reprennent aux choses dignes:
vent
pierres

loin de l'homme

si ce n'est l'allégeance universelle du désir.

Et le visage en sang
quelquefois
participe à la tendresse du soleil.   (OO, 124)

1988 sees the publication of two poetic collections, the short *Végétales* to which I shall return, and *Opéra des limites*, which precedes *Végetales* by a month and, in scope, ampleness and consistent vigour, is the equal, yet extension of *Opportunité des oiseaux*. A poem such as "Hors" (OL, 20) in many ways gives the measure of the work of this period as a whole, during which Marie-Claire Bancquart seems to look outside her own psychological and spiritual confines, and those of most of her fellow human beings--though only seemingly, for all is projection and will--in order to see in, for example, that "infinitive et douce / parole de forêt / vendange des sucs dans la terre", the ontological power and inspiration that can wilt within. There, visible, experienceable, actual, is the compassion the dream, the exquisite ephemeral presence, the endless imbrication, the enacted principle of love, that allows us to remember feasible bliss. "Couché à moitié hors de soi", she concludes, "on est une seconde d'arbre heureux". A poem like "Paix" (OL, 81), on the other hand, whilst amply echoing the immediate and potential meaning for us of externally projected symbols--the dignity, purpose and serenity of "le lierre et la verveine / qui cherchent racine / dans ta bouche. // Navets et pommes / [qui] fléchissent sur la langue"--pushes further this logic in inviting us to deliberately "cause night to go astray. / Accomplish what awaited you / between birth and cremation". We are thus pressed not only to see the world, but to assume ethically and spiritually the personal meaning of such seeing, "kill[ing] the clumsy hour within you / that does not breathe in the anise curliness of fennel". In this action, we come to understand that the things of presence are in themselves, but, more, for us, as symbols for our own possible being, a kind of "postdated Genesis", as Bancquart delightfully puts it in the early "Mer" (OL, 12): presence becomes truly (our) live creation, now, but as a sign, too, of "un avenir

fugace [qui] nous éclaire" (OL, 19). The poem "Au crépuscule...", part
of the "Suite au dieu-lune", is worthy of our attention in this regard, and
emblematic:

> Au crépuscule
> se lève une incarnation de notre impalpable
> emblavure au monde.
>
> Abolie la distance entre nuage et nous.
>
> L'intimité du sang avec la sève
> se tisse à la lueur des meubles.
>
> Notre corps la fleur et le dieu
> tout est compact.   (OL, 90)

As dusk, and night, begin to settle upon us, a resurrection improbably
occurs: an awareness, and a living, of some ineffable germinative relation
of self to world. Where exile and exodus had earlier been stressed, now--
this is the logic of passing and transmutation--affinity, intimacy,
joinedness may be sensed, in the humblest of circumstances, and a
"compactness" (: a putting-, a dwelling-, and a covenanting- together) may
emerge of self, world and some otherness deemed sacred. The final *suite*
of the volume (OL, 98-103), assuming the latter's title, leaps beyond the
various contradictions, "accursedness" and blindness earlier detailed as in
other collections, preferring to emphasise the simple, easily bypassed
"choses de silence / [qui] nous habitent" (OL, 61). Thus, the earth
broadcasts, Bancquart entreats us to recollect, "une fable de paix secrète"
(OL, 100), but depends upon each of us for the receipt of the discreet
signs of its fabulation. "L'opéra des limites", she writes--the poem, the
music, "the act and the place" of our finiteness recognised to be plunged
into some sacred, mysterious, invisible depth--"resplendira de tous nos
essais incomplets: / les amours dans la roselière / les citrons près d'un
collier d'ambre" (OL, 100). Incompleteness will thus not mar such

accomplishment, such "compactness" as Marie-Claire Bancquart intuits, now and for the future: it is a part of all action, all celebration-in-instalments, and it is homologically related to life's becoming and teemingness: small acts and words, not just "contre une expansion du grand creux" (OL, 83), but seeking some reintegration with "the disaffected words of [some ancient and divine] celebration" (OL, 101).

Fastidious formal moulding of the poetic voice is manifestly not a feature of a writer whose attention takes her freely to the realms of ethics and psychology, spirituality and philosophy, but it is important to stress the global, perhaps visceral discipline that inhabits her work. Although different patterns may be observed in earlier collections--an analysis of *Projets alternés*, and *Votre visage jusqu'à l'os*, for example would reveal marked distinctions in length and structure of poem--a considerable will for consistency remains always evident within a given collection, a constancy that is reflected, differently, in the later work of *Opéra des limites, Végétales* and *Sans lieu sinon l'attente*. The eloquently compact *Végétales*, for example, to which I should like now to give brief attention, provides seventeen texts, four in prose, the others in free verse (one combining the modes) revealing a very marked predilection for the 11 to 17 line poem and syllable count per line ranging from 2 to 17. These patterns are further harmonised by the noticeable regularity within variation of stanzaic structure, where 1-line, 2-line, 3-line and 4-line arrangements predominate. To some very considerable degree both *Opéra des limites* and *Sans lieu sinon l'attente* espouse all of these formal modalities: length of poem, stanzaic organisation and syllable count per line, whilst offering fluctuation both via the use of occasional prose texts and in pushing poem length either to more expansive measures (*Opéra des limites*, 22-, 24-, 29-, 44-line texts) or to occasionally telescoped

141

miniatures (*Sans lieu sinon l'attente*, 3-, 4-, 6-line texts). This said, however--and much more could be added on syntax and rhetoric--no aesthetic preciousness can be said to prevail: form, with Bancquart, weds thought with a mixture of spontaneity and vigilance, moulding its unfoldment with pertinence and elegant efficiency.

Much of *Végétales* articulates a need, personal and planetary, to open the self to its forgotten spaces, gardens, sun, inconspicuous germinating and growing things, and sense the linkedness of all phenomena, the "music" available via the intervals of being where "lack" may be felt to reign (V, 9). This harmony-within-infinite difference comes from Bancquart's developing intuition of "un dieu majeur [qui] épie la ténèbre des choses" (V, 9), a global "divineness" giving back to the seeming minima of existence their occulted maximality, showing that those "archipels dans l'irréparable de nous" (V, 15) are fragmentary, fleeting experiences and sensations whose meaning is yet to be trusted. If flowers and plants and the insects that hover about them, are the *blasons* of Bancquart's poetics, its corresponding mythical emblem is Osiris: "je parle Osiris, je suis Osiris" (V, 19), she maintains: murdered and resurrected goddess and muse of a culture of earth, growth and artistic endeavour. "Frôler avec l'abeille du baiser aveugle / mon pays ramassé dans un simulacre" (V, 20): such a poetic (: *simulacrum*: representation, *pictura/poiesis*) brushing against and fertilisation of the world may lead to a somewhat Ponge-like "espèce de joie" (V, 20), a liberation of that "parole d'ange" the things of existence may fragrantly give off (V, 23). Such a natural, though poetically, humanly converted, translated language can be suffused with that love that, beyond truth and falsehood, does not cease to call out to us (V, 26). The closing poem, "Devant l'eau illisible" (V, 28-9) certainly shows that tensions remain in the newly tempered soft

142

steeliness of Bancquart's poetics, but the overall tone of *Végétales*, as with the contemporary *Opéra des limites*, is one of increasingly risked intuition of the new creative dimensions of sensation, emotion and meditation.

Sans lieu sinon l'attente (1991) constitutes an important and substantial extension of the thrust of Marie-Claire Bancquart's poetic *œuvre*. Articulated in six parts--"Paroles de la femme", "Domaine bas", "A la merveille", "Intimité des os", "Vous devenez une île heureuse" and "Entre les yeux nus de Dieu""--the collection generates a powerful expression of the peaking vastness yet concentration of the poet's at once visionary and firmly anchored undertaking. "De la rose à l'inadmissible / l'espace étroit comme une trace d'ange / est arpenté par le poète" (SL, 114). Meaning can thus be questioned yet attached to the obscure, the anonymous, the unseen, the wasteful (SL, 30); Bancquart knows that the "hymns" of the earth are not "begun" by us, may perhaps lie beyond all origin, being intrinsic, immanent (SL, 45); and she knows, too, that our search for the language of being's unity (SL, 56), like our approach to being, is caught in the tensions of embrace and a *dérive* yet *matricielle*, of a sense of dwelling and a psychology of erosion (SL, 65). Fissure and "vehement" presence thus divide--and join--our reflections and our emotions (SL, 69); meaning, warmth, allegiance, even blatancy, thus wrestle with factors of illusion and fleetingness (SL, 99); our 'place'--our "place and our act" (V, 17)--is one of waiting, expectation, for some intuited angelicalness, our believing inadequately matching our seeing. I conclude by offering for further meditation, the aptly titled poem, "Tacite" which conveys eloquently the rich ampleness of a very fine poet's inner debate:

143

Fidèle à la verdeur qui veille en la cerise
notre coeur
lavé dans le soir
hiberne l'énigme.

On ne commence pas les hymnes.

On attend que la nuit exaltant le pain sur la table
rassemble le goût de l'été.

Dans une obscurité de bouche
toutes les rumeurs se recueillent.

Le poivron frais l'olive
deviennent offrande
pour le dieu pressenti.   (SL, 45)

AN INTERIM CONCLUSION

Une femme créait le soleil
En elle
Et ses mains étaient belles
La terre plongeait sous ses pieds
Joyce Mansour

Femmes à la chevelure nocturne --
Incendiées! -- Doubles! -- Téméraires!
-- Folles!
Marianne van Hirtum

Croyez moi, je n'ai jamais agi sans
salut
Danielle Sarrera

The extreme provisionality of these concluding remarks will, I hope, be readily understandable. It is not just a question of procrastination, pleasurable as all procrastination is; nor do I seek to avoid the difficulties of chiasmic summary, real though they seem to me. Nor is brevity to be laid at the door of an admittedly avowed preference for the intensity of individually focussed studies, for I recognise too the need to see what, globally, interpertinently, may be argued over and above the teeming specificities determined. On the other hand, it is important to stress that the latter, for me, remain the principal accomplishment to date, an accomplishment of personal discovery in eight parts. Moreover, whilst I shall now add a few further remarks, gathering singlenesses into the elements of some shared poetics, the latter's provisionality stems from my residual and authentic desire to await still a larger gathering, when, at the close of the second volume of *Contemporary French Women Poets*, I can draw upon the full range of some sixteen feminine literary practices. This, I trust, in compensation, may permit a coordination more purposeful, more meditated, more nuanced. What the preceding pages may have achieved, demonstrate, I hope sufficiently, that what Mary Daly called the "wip[ing] out of women's questions [under patriarchy]" has been in turn, in some small measure, further erased. Any globalising conclusions may, moreover, however interesting, not quite equal the attention we can ever offer to one given feminine *œuvre*. And, I still tend to persist in the view that conclusions risk closing off more than they open up...

This said, let me suggest that, in the eight *œuvres* examined to this point, there is an argument to be made for the need to distinguish, subtly, between the will to intellectualise experience and the desire to verbalise the latter in poetic terms. The poets we have looked at in this volume-- even Anne Teyssiéras in her *Clavicules de Minho*, Andrée Chedid in texts like "Chantier du poème" or "Epreuves de l'écrit", or Marie-Claire Bancquart in rare commentaries upon *her own* personal poetics--all tend to eschew the reductive rationalisation of the real. Their preference goes, not to some *surdétermination* of the language they use and the constructions it inevitably generates, but rather to a couching of the lived within a language unpretentious in its felt fragileness yet honoured in the openness, the relative freedom of its antitheoretical, anticonceptualising gesture. "L'abeille qui se pose sur la rose... donne vie à la légende", writes Françoise Mallet-Joris: experience animating concept, not theory, pure "legend" as an *a priori* to experience and its opaque, transparent infinity. Literary conceit thus plays fourth fiddle to a saying that knows of the deep unsaids and unsayables haunting experience. If this first point might be thought to downplay the value of the language of women, it must be appreciated that exactly the opposite effect is in fact achieved. For--and this is my second point--the language of experience, that "musique pour les sourds" as Catherine Fauln once called it, involves a direct speaking

146

of woman's desire--"[sa] passion perdue [enfin] permise", writes Anne Hébert--and this, precisely non-oblique, because non-methodologised or little theorised, speaking of desire constitutes, to my mind, that very "revolution" that Catherine Clément felt could not be achieved at such a "level"--but which Hélène Cixous understands to be critical to feminine transformation of being. The point is well made by Josephine Donovan, who argues the entrapments for feminist criticism--an argument I shall extend to women's creative writing as a whole--of theory, obscurantist intellectualisation and the decentralising thrust of a deconstruction leading, as Terry Eagleton suggests, to possible "quietism". "Vis sans peur, sans remords et sans contrainte", Anna de Noailles advises. And, indeed, the fundamental agendas of these women poets are, in short, always their own, and, crucially visceral, affective, they are far from being purely notional, essentialising, platonic. "Bouche pour te maudire", wrote Louise Ackermann in Verlaine's time, and speaking of male war, "et cœur pour t'exécrer".

This, however, thirdly, is far from suggesting either that the poets dealt with here retire into some cosy esotericism, some involuted mental privacy, or that they, in their consciousness of the unsaids and unsayables of the real, angle mind and heart towards varyingly defined strictly subjective transcendences. On the contrary, all eight women, from Chedid and Mitaud to Risset and Bancquart, remain, and indeed become increasingly with the years, exquisitely sensitive to the daily traumas and sufferings as well as the flashing and still stunningly available joys of the world, its minima, its throbbing options, its dark yet lighted enigmaticalness. Such vast experience, immediate and vicarious--"présence inexorable... / Tu me tires d'un long et morne enchantement", writes Catherine Fauln--, is thus a central agent of consciousness-raising, but, equally, it is persistently seen in the perspective of a non-verbalness--the myriad epiphenomena of heart and soul, desire and intuition--that poetry in a sense inevitably tends to emblematise. If, then, the miseries and wants articulated in the 1987 *U.N. Decade for Women* are only too well sensed by a Denise Le Dantec or an Anne Teyssiéras, they do not block off mental, emotional and spiritual--I use the term in its broadest connotation--avenues and *cheminements*. What may be termed feminine struggle--and, if Marceline Desbordes-Valmore saw quickly the "nobility" of all struggle inspired by love, her daughter Ondine could be plunged into the depths of despair and impasse so many women still terribly know: "je ne lutterai pas, regretteuse asservie / Que je suis"--struggle, then, may be painfully pragmatic, but it may too imply a *cheminement* of non-verbal spiritual accomplishment so central to our (well-)being, so readily parenthesised in "masculine" thought and action.

To think, then--it is my fourth point in this provisional reflection--of the other, is to accomplish simultaneously two things for the women I have spoken of. It is, on the one hand, to remain lucidly open to multiplicity, diversity, human and non-human presence in its endless difference and becoming; on the other --but it is only the other side of the same hand, in effect--it is to realise the profound otherness ever, and teemingly, available in being and our experience--the receipt, characterisation, determination and, even, improbably, choice, thereof. Distance and nearness thus can merge their optics both on the level of observation and that of vision. The seemingly endless violations of our collective integrity do not obviate a shared poetics of possible, indeed real, esteem. "C'est bien vous que j'aime si je m'aime", Marie Nizet reminds us. Fear can be, is, met with a logic of love at times astonishing in its resilience, even its naturalness, its bizarre confidence. What Nicole

Brossard terms "l'insoutenable posture discursive" can thus at least be countered by a relation permitting "[à] chaque femme [de] répéter son histoire au moins une fois dans sa vie comme un mot d'esprit, avec la passion de son espoir". This poetics of relationship-to-other(ness) related, translated, let me stress once more, is performed without angelicising evasion, without idealisation, though its dogged courage or serene trust do, via a process of self-projection, visualise, en-vision a self-other renewal and transmutation of impressive proportions. One could argue here, in this envisioning that disturbs and reshapes self and other, what Sally Minogue would consider the intrinsic "polemicalness" of feminist, perhaps all women's, poetry, whether the polemics be overt or more secretly subversive, more quietly transformational. But, equally, one could stress, with Simone Weil, a profound sense of the ever-remaining "caress" of day within day's blatant contradictions.

A fifth and final point, very much linked to the preceding remarks. Women's poetry is not ideology. It implies no fixity of system. I am not just thinking here of aesthetics or underpinning literary theory. This was the object of my first remark. But nothing about the work of Chedid or Dohollau, Mitaud or Tellermann, anchors itself in prescription nor indeed proscription. The poems of Bancquart lie open, exposed, prone, candidly proffered. Their openness may be one of vision, but it is, too, an openness entailing question, uncertainty, opaqueness. The "je ne sais..." of a Catherine Pozzi ("Nyx") mirrors Duras' endless unknowings and Bancquart's searching anti-ideology. Just as no definitive claims attach to language, no power, no "having" clutter the notional realms beyond language. In a sense, then, relativity and problematicalness persist at the heart of any 'chiasmic" poetics we may glimpse in reading the eight *œuvres* orienting this study: but this relativity is the openness of being itself, a being never to be "had", constantly becoming, a state and an action of otherness now defined as utter frustration, not to say torment, now as swarming option, real future. "Tes paroles conduisent où elles n'existent pas", as Annie Salager puts it.

SELECTED BIBLIOGRAPHY

ACKERMANN, LOUISE. *Oeuvres de Madame Ackermann.* Paris. Lemerre. 1885.

ARTAUD, ANTONIN. *L'Ombilic des limbes.* Paris: Gallimard. 1968.

BLANCQUART, MARIE-CLAIRE. *Projets alternés.* Mortemart: Rougerie. 1972.

_____. *Mains dissoutes.* Mortemart: Rougerie. 1975.

_____. *Mémoire d'abolie.* Paris: Belfond. 1978.

_____. *Partition.* Paris: Belfond. 1981.

_____. *Voix.* St. Laurent du Pont: Le Verbe et l'Empreinte. 1979.

_____. *Votre visage jusqu'à l'os.* Paris: Temps actuels. 1983.

_____. *Opportunité des oiseaux.* Paris: Belfond. 1986.

_____. *Végétales.* Montereau: Les Cahiers du Confluent. 1988.

_____. *Opéra des limites.* Paris: Corti 1988.

_____. *Sans lieu sinon l'attente.* Paris: Obsidiane. 1991.

BARTHES, ROLAND. *Le Degré zéro de l'écriture, suivi de Nouveaux essais critiques.* Paris: Seuil. 1972.

BAUDELAIRE, CHARLES. *Oeuvres complètes.* Paris: Gallimard. Pléiade. 1961.

BERSIANIK, LOUKY. *La Main tranchante du symbole.* Montréal: Remue-Ménage. 1980.

BISHOP, MICHAEL. *The Contemporary Poetry of France. Eight Studies.* Amsterdam: Rodopi. 1985.

_____. *Nineteenth-Century French Poetry.* New York: Twayne. 1993.

_____. "Trois voix contemporaines: Risset, Le Dantec, Tellermann", in *Thirty Voices in the Feminine*, ed. M. Bishop. Amsterdam: Rodopi. 1995.

_____. "Contemporary Women Poets", in *Contemporary French Poetry*, ed. R. Stamelman, Special issue of *Studies in Twentieth-Century Literature*, Winter 1989.

_____. "De Denise Le Dantec à Marie Etienne: passion, sérénité, profondeur", in *Simone de Beauvoir et les féminismes contemporains*, Special issue of *Dalhousie French Studies*, Fall-Winter 1987.

_____. "L'Année poétique: De Guillevic, Deguy et Jaccottet à Tellermann, Etienne et Baude", *French Review*, October 1994.

BONNEFOY, YVES. *Début et fin de la neige.* Paris: Mercure de France. 1991.

_____. *Le Nuage rouge.* Paris: Mercure de France, 1993.

151

_____. *La Vie errante*. Paris: Mercure de France, 1993.

BRINDEAU, SERGE. *La Poésie contemporaine de langue française depuis 1945*. Paris: Saint-Germain-des-Prés. 1973.

BROOME, PETER and GRAHAM CHESTERS. *The Appreciation of Modern French Poetry 1850-1950*. Cambridge U.P. 1976.

BROSSARD, NICOLE. *La Lettre aérienne*. Montréal: Remue-Ménage. 1985.

CARDINAL, ROGER, ed. *Sensibility and Creation*. London: Croom Helm. 1977.

CHAR, RENÉ. *Oeuvres complètes*. Paris: Gallimard. Pléiade. 1983.

_____. *Éloge d'une Soupçonnée*. Paris: Gallimard. 1988.

CAWS, MARY ANN. *A Metapoetics of the Passage*. U.P. of New England. 1981.

CHEDID, ANDRÉE. *Textes pour une figure*. Paris: Pré aux Clercs. 1949.

_____. *Textes pour un poème (1949-1970)*. Paris: Flammarion. 1987.

_____. *Poèmes pour un texte (1970-1991)*. Paris: Flammarion. 1991.

_____. *7 plantes pour un herbier*. (Bédée): Folle Avoine. 1985.

_____. *Textes pour un poème*. Paris: G.L.M. 1950.

_____. *Textes pour le vivant*. Paris: G.L.M. 1953.

_____. *Textes pour la terre aimée*. Paris: G.L.M. 1955.

_____. *Terre et poésie*. Paris: G.L.M. 1956.

_____. *Terre regardée*. Paris: G.L.M. 1957.

_____. *Seul, le visage*. Paris: G.L.M. 1960

_____. *Double-pays*. Paris: G.L.M. 1965

_____. *Contre-chant* Paris: Flammarion. 1969.

_____. *Visage premier*. Paris: Flammarion. 1972.

_____. *Fraternité de la parole*. Paris: Flammarion. 1976.

_____. *Cavernes et soleils*. Paris: Flammarion. 1979.

_____. *Fêtes et lubies*. Paris: Flammarion. 1973.

_____. *Cérémonial de la violence*. Paris: Flammarion. 1976.

_____. *Épreuves du vivant*. Paris: Flammarion. 1983.

CIXOUS, HÉLÈNE. *Jours de l'an*. Paris: Des Femmes. 1990.

_____. *Le livre de Promethea*. Paris: Gallimard. 1983.

_____. *Manne*. Paris: Des Femmes. 1988.

DALY, MARY. *Beyond God the Father*. Boston: Beacon. 1973.

_____. *Gyn/ecology: The Metaethics of Radical Feminism*. Boston: Beacon. 1978.

DEGUY, MICHEL. *Actes*. Paris: Gallimard. 1966.

_____. *Gisants*. Paris: Gallimard. 1985.

_____. *Aux heures d'affluence*. Paris: Seuil. 1993.

_____. *A ce qui n'en finit pas*. Paris: Seuil. 1995.

DERRIDA, JACQUES. *Margins of Philosophy.* U. Chicago P. 1982.

_____. *Positions.* U. Chicago P. 1981.

DESBORDES-VALMORE, MARCELINE. *Poésies.* Paris: Gallimard. 1983.

DELVAILLE, BERNARD. *La Nouvelle Poésie.* Paris: Seghers. 1974.

DELUY, HENRY. *Poésie en France. 1983-1988. Une anthologie critique.* Paris: Flammarion. 1989.

DOHOLLAU, HEATHER. *Seule enfance.* Privas: Solaire. 1978.

_____. *La Venelle des portes.* (Bédée): Folle Avoine. 1980.

_____. *La Réponse.* (Bédée): Folle Avoine. 1982.

_____. *L'Adret du jour.* (Bédée): Folle Avoine. 1989.

_____. *Les Portes d'en bas.* Bédée: Folle Avoine. 1992.

_____. *Matière de lumière.* (Bédée): Folle Avoine. 1985.

_____. *Pages aquarellées.* (Bédée): Folle Avoine. 1989.

DONOVAN, JOSEPHINE, ed. *Feminist Literary Criticism.* Lexington:.U P. Kentucky. 1989.

DUCHEN, CLAIRE, ed. *French Connections.* Univ. Massachusetts P. 1987.

DU BOUCHET, ANDRÉ. *L'Incohérence.* Paris: Hachette. 1979.

_____. *Carnets 1952-1958.* Paris: Plon. 1990.

DU GUILLET, PERNETTE. *Poésies.* Geneva: Slatkine. 1970.

DUPIN, JACQUES. *Dehors.* Paris: Gallimard. 1975.

_____. *Échancré.* Paris: P.O.L. 1991.

EAGLETON, MARY, ed. *Feminist Literary Criticism.* London/New York: Longman. 1991.

ELUARD, PAUL. *Oeuvres complètes.* Paris: Gallimard. Pléiade. 1968.

FAULN, CATHERINE. *Fenêtres sur le paradis.* Author. 1946.

_____. *Les Éphémères.* Author. c. 1950.

FETZER, GLENN. "Avènement de la parole: illusion et réalité chez Anne Teyssiéras et Céline Zins", in *Thirty Voices in the Feminine,* Amsterdam: Rodopi. 1995.

FRANKLIN, SARAH. *Luce Irigaray and the Feminist Critique of Language.* Univ. Kent, Canterbury. 1985.

FRASER, ARVONNE. *The U.N. Decade for Women.* Boulder/London: Westview P. 1987.

FRÉNAUD, ANDRÉ. *La Sorcière de Rome.* Paris: Gallimard. 1973.

_____. *Nul ne s'égare.* Paris: Gallimard. 1986.

_____. *Notre inhabileté fatale.* Paris: Gallimard. 1979.

GATENS, MOIRA. *Feminism and Philosophy.* Indiana U.P. 1991.

GLEIZE, JEAN-MARIE. *A noir. Poésie et littéralité.* Paris: Seuil. 1992.

GROULT, BENOITE. *Ainsi soit-elle.* Paris: Grasset. 1975.

GREENE, ROBERT. *Six French Poets of Our Time*. Princeton U.P. 1979.

HIRTUM, MARIANNE VAN. *Les Insolites*. Paris: Gallimard. 1956.

_____. *Poèmes pour les petits pauvres*. Paris: Seghers. 1956.

HUGO, VICTOR. *Les Contemplations*. Paris: Le Livre de Poche. 1964.

_____. *La Légende des siècles*. 2 vols. Paris: Garnier-Flammarion. 1967.

_____. *Poésie. III*. Paris: Seuil. 1971.

HYVRARD, JEANNE. *Le Silence et l'obscurité*. Paris: Montalba. 1982.

_____. *Le Corps défunt de la comédie*. Paris: Seuil. 1982.

HÉBERT, ANNE. *Poèmes*. Paris: Seuil. 1960.

IRIGARAY, LUCE. *Ce sexe qui n'en est pas un*. Paris: Minuit. 1977.

_____. *Parler n'est jamais neutre*. Paris. Minuit. 1985.

JABÈS, EDMOND. *Ça suit son cours*. (Montpellier): Fata Morgana. 1975.

_____. *Le Seuil; le sable; poésies complètes*. Paris: Gallimard. 1990.

JACCOTTET, PHILIPPE. *Cahier de verdure*. Paris: Gallimard. 1990.

_____. *Cristal et fumée*. Saint-Clément-la-Rivière: Fata Morgana. 1993.

_____. *Beauregard*. Paris: Maeght. 1981.

KNAPP, BETTINA. *Andrée Chedid*. Amsterdam: Rodopi. 1984.

LABÉ, LOUISE. *Oeuvres complètes*. Geneva: Droz. 1981.

LA CHARITÉ, VIRGINIA. *Twentieth-Century French Avant-Garde Poetry, 1907-1990*. Lexington: French Forum. 1992.

LACAN, JACQUES. *Écrits*. Paris: Seuil. 1966-71.

LAUTRÉAMONT. *Oeuvres complètes*. Paris: Corti. 1969.

LE DANTEC, DENISE. *Métropole*. Honfleur: Oswald. 1970.

_____. *Le Bar aux oiseaux*. Libretto. Création. 1980.

_____. *Mémoire des dunes*. (Bédée): Folle Avoine. 1985.

_____. *Les Fileuses d'étoupe*. (Bédée): Folle Avoine. 1985.

_____. *Opuscule d'Ouessant*. Paris: Babel. 1992.

_____. *Le Jour*. Paris: Des Femmes. 1975.

_____. *Les Joueurs de Go*. Paris: Stock. 1977.

_____. *Le Journal des roses*. Paris: Bourin. 1991.

_____. *Suite pour une enfance*. Paris: Des Femmes. 1992.

_____. *Le Roman des jardins de France*. Paris: Plon. 1987.

_____. *La Vie déserte et quelques lieux*. (Bédée): Folle Avoine. 1990.

_____. "Champ-Bretagne", in *La Bretagne*. Chavagne: Ubacs, 1987.

LAMARTINE, ALPHONSE DE. *Oeuvres complètes*. Paris: Gallimard. Pléiade. 1963.

LEUWERS, DANIEL. *Introduction à la poésie moderne et contemporaine*. Paris: Bordas. 1990.

MALLET-JORIS, FRANÇOISE. *Poèmes du dimanche*. Brussels: Edns des Artistes. 1947.

———. *Trois âges de la nuit*. Paris: Grasset. 1968.

MALLARMÉ, STÉPHANE. *Oeuvres complètes*. Paris: Gallimard. Pléiade. 1945.

———. *Pour un tombeau d'Anatole*. Paris: Seuil. 1961.

MICHAUX, HENRI. *Déplacements dégagements*. Paris: Gallimard. 1985.

———. *Chemins cherchés Chemins perdus Transgressions*. Paris: Gallima. d. 1982.

MANSOUR, JOYCE. *Cris*. Paris: Seghers. 1953.

———. *Ça!* Paris: Le Soleil Noir. 1970.

MINOGUE, SALLY, ed. *Problems for Feminist Criticism*. London/New York: Routledge. 1990.

MITAUD, JANINE. *L'Échange des colères*. (Mortemart): Rougerie. 1965.

———. *Hâte de vivre*. Paris: Seghers. 1949.

———. *Départs*. Paris: Seghers. 1952.

———. *Bras étendus*. Paris: Monteiro. 1951.

———. *Silence fabuleux*. St. Jouin de Marne: Signe du Temps. 1951.

———. *La Porte de la terre*. (Mortemart): Rougerie. 1969.

———. *La Parole naturelle*. Paris: Métamorphoses. 1971.

———. *Danger*. Mortemart: Rougerie. 1974.

———. *Le Soleil sursoit*. Périgueux: Fanlac. 1974.

———. *Livre-poème*. Périgueux: Fanlac. 1979.

———. *Suite baroque*. Périgueux: Fanlac. 1983.

———. *De la rose à l'éros*. Paris: Chambelland. 1982.

———. *Poèmes cruels*. Mortemart: Rougerie. 1988.

———. *Pages*. Mortemart: Rougerie. 1991.

MOI, TORIL. *French Feminist Thought: A Reader*. Oxford: Blackwell. 1987.

MOULIN, JEANINE. *La Pierre à feux*. Paris: Seghers. 1968.

———. *Huit siècles de poésie féminine. Anthologie*. Paris: Seghers. 1963.

NIZET, MARIE. *Pour Axel de Missie*. Brussels: Vie Intellectuelle. 1923.

NOAILLES, ANNA DE. *Le Coeur innombrable*. Paris: Calmann-Lévy. 1901.

———. *Les Vivants et les morts*. Paris: Fayard. 1913.

———. *Derniers vers et poèmes d'enfance*. Paris: Grasset. 1934.

NOËL, BERNARD. *L'Été langue morte*. Saint-Clément-la-Rivière: Fata Morgana. 1976.

———. *La Chute des temps*. Paris: Gallimard. 1993.

NOËL, MARIE. *Les Chansons et les heures*. Paris: Sansot. 1920.
_____. *Le Rosaire des joies*. Paris: Crès. 1930.
OLLENBURGER, JANE. *A Sociology of Women*. New Jersey: Prentice Hall. 1992.
PONGE, FRANCIS. *La Rage de l'expression*. Paris: Gallimard. 1976.
_____. *Le Parti pris des choses*. Paris: Gallimard. 1967.
_____. *Comment une figue de paroles et pourquoi*. Paris: Flammarion. 1977.
POZZI, CATHERINE. *Poèmes*. Paris: N.R.F. 1959.
REVERDY, PIERRE. *Note éternelle du présent*. Paris: Flammarion. 1973.
_____. *Cette émotion appelée poésie*. Paris: Flammarion. 1974.
RICHARD, JEAN-PIERRE. *Onze études sur la poésie moderne*. Paris: Seuil. 1964.
RIMBAUD, ARTHUR. *Oeuvres complètes*. Paris: Gallimard. Pléiade. 1963.
RISSET, JACQUELINE. *Jeu*. Paris: Seuil. 1971.
_____. *L'Anagramme du désir*. Rome: Bulzoni. 1971.
_____. *La Traduction commence*. Paris: Bourgois. 1976.
_____. *Sept passages de la vie d'une femme*. Paris: Flammarion. 1985.
_____. *L'Amour de loin*. Paris: Flammarion. 1989.
_____. *Petits éléments de physique amoureuse*. Paris: Gallimard. 1991.
ROCHE, DENIS. *Le Mécrit*. Paris: Seuil. 1972.
_____. *Louve basse*. Paris: Seuil. 1976.
ROUSSELOT, JEAN. *Poètes français d'aujourd'hui*. Paris: Seghers: 1965.
SALAGER, ANNIE. *La Femme-buisson*. Paris: Saint-Germain-des-Prés. 1973.
SARRERA, DANIELLE. "L'Ostiaque", in *Poètes singuliers du surréalisme et autres lieux*. Paris: U.G.E. 1971.
SEGHERS, PIERRE. *Le Livre d'or de la poésie française*. Paris: Seghers. 1969.
SELLERS, SUSAN. *Feminist Criticism*. Univ. Toronto P. 1991.
STAMELMAN, RICHARD. *Lost Beyond Telling*. Ithaca: Cornell U.P. 1990.
STEINMETZ, JEAN-LUC. *La Poésie et ses raisons*. Paris: Corti. 1990.
TELLERMANN, ESTHER. *Première apparition avec épaisseur*. Paris: Flammarion. 1986.
_____. *Trois plans inhumains*. Paris: Flammarion. 1989.
_____. *Distance de fuite*. Paris: Flammarion. 1993.

TEYSSIÉRAS, ANNE. *Épervier ma solitude*. Mortemart: Rougerie. 1966.

_____. *Le Chemin sous la mer*. Mortemart: Rougerie. 1992.

_____. *Fragments pour une captive*. Mortemart: Rougerie. 1969.

_____. *Cinq étapes pour une attente*. Mortemart: Rougerie. 1971.

_____. *Dernier état*. Mortemart: Rougerie. 1974.

_____. *L'Écaille des eaux*. Mortemart: Rougerie. 1975.

_____. *Parallèles*. Mortemart: Rougerie. 1976.

_____. *Le Pays d'où j'irai*. Mortemart: Rougerie. 1977.

_____. *Juste avant la nuit*. Mortemart: Rougerie. 1979.

_____. *Boule de cristal*. Mortemart: Rougerie. 1982.

_____. *Les Clavicules de Minho*. Mortemart: Rougerie. 1986.

_____. *Poèmes en Kabbale*. Mortemart: Rougerie. 1984.

_____. *Instants pour la seconde vie*. Mortemart: Rougerie. 1994.

VALMORE, ONDINE. *Les Cahiers de Ondine Valmore*. Paris: Ch. Bosse. 1932.

WEIL, SIMONE. *La Connaissance surnaturelle*. Paris: N.R.F. 1950.

_____. "Poèmes", *Lettres Françaises*. 29.xi.62.

WILSON, KATHARINA. *An Encyclopedia of Continental Women Writers*. Volume One: A-K; Volume Two: L-Z. New York: Garland. 1991.